A PASSION FOR IGNORANCE

A Passion for Ignorance

WHAT WE CHOOSE NOT TO KNOW AND WHY

RENATA SALECL

PRINCETON UNIVERSITY PRESS

PRINCETON & OXFORD

Published by Princeton University Press
41 William Street, Princeton, New Jersey 08540
6 Oxford Street, Woodstock, Oxfordshire OX20 1TR

press.princeton.edu

Library of Congress Cataloging-in-Publication Data

Names: Salecl, Renata, 1962– author.
Title: A passion for ignorance : what we choose not to know and why /
    Renata Salecl.
Description: Princeton : Princeton University Press, 2020. | Includes
    bibliographical references and index.
Identifiers: LCCN 2020022587 (print) | LCCN 2020022588 (ebook) |
    ISBN 9780691195605 (hardback) | ISBN 9780691202020 (ebook)
Subjects: LCSH: Ignorance (Theory of knowledge)—Social aspects.
Classification: LCC BD221 .S25 2020 (print) | LCC BD221 (ebook) |
    DDC 302/.17—dc23
LC record available at https://lccn.loc.gov/2020022587
LC ebook record available at https://lccn.loc.gov/2020022588

British Library Cataloging-in-Publication Data is available

Editorial: Sarah Caro, Rob Tempio, Josh Drake, and Matt Rohal
Production Editorial: Natalie Baan
Jacket Design: Leslie Flis
Production: Erin Suydam
Publicity: Kate Farquhar-Thomson and Sara Henning-Stout
Copyeditor: Ashley Moore

Jacket images: Head in sand, Jan-Otto/iStock; Sky, Shutterstock

This book has been composed in Arno Pro with Avenir LT Std Display

Printed on acid-free paper. ∞

Printed in the United States of America

10 9 8 7 6 5 4 3 2 1

For Branko

CONTENTS

A PASSION FOR IGNORANCE

Introduction

IN MARCH 2020, as the coronavirus crisis started hitting the United States, the *Financial Times* published a cartoon by James Ferguson showing President Donald Trump sitting in the Oval Office with a surgical mask over his eyes and his hands clamped firmly over his ears. On the floor, a picture shows Chinese president Xi Jinping wearing a surgical mask made from the Chinese flag. While one leader is closing his eyes and ears, the other's mouth is covered by the symbols of country and ideology. The spreading of the virus has presented the world with its biggest challenge in dealing with the unknown in a century. Ignorance, denial, and negation all played their part at the start of the pandemic, as highlighted in extreme relief by the behavior of the US president. At first, Trump ignored the danger of the infection spreading in the United States. In January and February 2020, when coronavirus was propagating rapidly around the world, Trump claimed that there was no need for concern in the United States because there were only a few people infected, and they had all come from abroad. In denial of events as they unfolded, he assured the public that "everything is under control," that "the new virus is not more dangerous than the flu," and that he had a "natural capacity" to understand the infection. When it became impossible to continue ignoring the pandemic, Trump changed tack, and this time declared a "war" against the "invisible enemy." The president did not recognize the severity of the situation because he was suddenly convinced by the experts, or because he had new information; rather, he told the public he had known all along how serious it was: "I felt it was a pandemic long before it was called a pandemic." He then added, "But we are going to defeat the invisible enemy. I think we are going to do it even faster than we thought, and it'll be a complete victory. It'll be a total victory."[1]

A decade previously, the writers of *The Simpsons* had imagined a drug that induced a similar degree of blind optimism. In a well-known episode, Lisa has to give a presentation at school on what Springfield will look like in fifty years' time. Diligent as ever, she immerses herself in climate change research and presents a grim outlook for her hometown. Her presentation is so frightening that her teachers urge her parents to have her assessed by a psychiatrist. After the examination, the doctor diagnoses Lisa with environment-related despair and prescribes her a drug called Ignorital. With the help of this drug, Lisa's perception of the world changes; released from despair, she becomes overwhelmingly optimistic. Clouds appear to her as smiling teddy bears, and she continuously hears in her head the song "What a Wonderful World." Lisa's parents struggle to cope with this optimistic delirium and decide to take her off Ignorital. Marge and Homer realize that the old, pessimistic Lisa was easier to handle than the madly cheerful one.

The idea that a drug or some other form of treatment might help us ignore those parts of reality we find hard to bear is not confined to fiction. For decades, science has tried to find a way to subdue the traumatic memories of war veterans or victims of other violence. These studies sometimes suggest that a drug that allows someone to forget traumatic violence might be of special help to those who have been raped or suffered terrifying assault or sexual abuse. The ethical debates surrounding the use of drugs or other means to alleviate memories of violence often focus on whether it is possible or desirable to erase only selected parts of the memory and what would happen if the perpetrators of violent crimes or abuse could access such memory-eliminating drugs to escape being identified or persecuted. Yet even without such drugs, people find ways to ignore, deny, or negate knowledge that threatens their well-being.

Each epoch is marked by its own ignorance. The way people relate to knowledge is highly contextual; and what is considered to be knowledge is not only socially constructed but also highly individual. To complicate things further, people often embrace ignorance or denial (which, as we shall see later, are not the same thing) when they come close to knowledge that is somehow unbearable.

The French psychoanalyst Jacques Lacan borrowed the term "a passion for ignorance," found in Buddhist studies, to describe how his patients did everything they could to avoid acknowledging the cause of their suffering, even though most of them came to him claiming that they wanted to understand it. Lacan also looked at ignorance on the side of the analyst and concluded that the analyst should not take the position of "the one who knows the answers," but rather should embrace the position of nonknowledge and allow analysands to discover for themselves what underlay their symptoms.

This book will explore the nature of the passion for ignorance. On the one hand it will examine how we try to avoid dealing with traumatic knowledge, and on the other hand it will analyze how societies find ever new ways to deny information that might undermine the power structures or ideological mechanisms that maintain the existing order. In addition, I will try to explain how in postindustrial, knowledge-based societies, the power of ignorance has acquired a surprising new strength, even as people can now learn more about each other and themselves than ever before with the help of science and new technology. The way we relate to knowledge is never neutral, which is why the term "passion," which *Merriam-Webster* defines as an "intense, driving, or overmastering feeling or conviction,"[2] can help us understand not only why people embrace what is perceived as truth but also why they ignore, deny, or negate it. Curiosity is for some a passion, and when people stop questioning established knowledge, the lack of this passion might very well open new doors to ignorance.[3]

The concept of ignorance needs to be reexamined because we are undergoing a revolutionary change in the nature of knowledge. The development of genetics, neuroscience, and big data has changed our understanding of what can be known about the individual. With new kinds of information come new anxieties, spurred by the difficulties in comprehending what this information means, by questions concerning who has access to it, and by concerns about who can use or manipulate it. The emergence of new types of information in the field of medicine means that the question of whether "to know or not to know" has become of vital importance for the individual. It is equally important that ignorance is examined in relation to new mechanisms of power. In the second half of the twentieth century, the French philosopher Michel Foucault wrote at length about the relation between power and knowledge; today, the relation between power and ignorance demands equal attention.

People have always found ways to close their eyes, ears, and mouths in order to ignore, deny, and negate information that they find disturbing. They will identify with a leader even if his or her discourse is full of lies. What is different in these "post-truth" times is the rise of "cognitive inertia"—an increase of indifference to what is truth and what is a lie. This indifference is linked to an inability to know and not a simple lack of willingness to learn. If we look at how "fake" news is transmitted via the internet, it is often difficult to identify its sources and not at all clear what it is trying to achieve. In August 2017, for example, a campaign on Twitter with the hashtag #borderfreecoffee created a fake promotion by Starbucks offering illegal immigrants a free Frappuccino in Starbucks coffee shops across America on a certain day. Starbucks worked hard to convince their customers that the offer was a hoax. Some people thought that it might have been created by pro-immigrant hackers. But in fact the opposite was true. The hoax was hatched by people opposed to immigration who thought it would be a great idea to entice illegal immigrants to a particular place and then, while they were waiting in line for a free drink, get the police to arrest them. While some fake news campaigns have an underlying political or economic agenda, many are simply tools to gather more clicks and thereby gain more advertising revenue. With the proliferation of fake news, it is not surprising that mistrust in all sources of news is on the rise. Indifference and ignorance in such cases act as a protective shield for the individual who is continuously having to assess what information to trust and what not to. As William Davis has noted, this becomes a serious political problem when people turn against all representations and framings of reality in the media, believing them all to be equally biased, because then they believe either that there is no truth or that there exists outside normal channels of political communication some purer, unmediated access to truth.[4]

In this book I will address two intimately related topics: not knowing (ignorance) and not acknowledging (ignoring). Both states of mind are hugely relevant to our society, our culture, and our intellectual life today. Ignorance and ignoring both present problems, and at times both have their uses and benefits. For example, ignorance presents a danger when it is treated as a virtue in itself, or if it is seen as a shameful state that we must strive to escape through consumption in the postmodern "knowledge economy." Conversely, ignorance provides a natural buffer as we strive to understand who we are and what our place in the world could be. Ignorance usefully marks the point where a professional's expertise can go no further; more profoundly, it sets a boundary to what we can reasonably expect of people, individually and collectively.

The act of ignoring something, consciously or unconsciously, takes a similarly diverse range of forms. Sometimes to deny what one patently sees may be a strategy[5] on which survival depends; at other times, denial perpetuates the collective fear on which abusive relationships and tyrannical hierarchies depend. But ignorance may also be a way of refusing to acknowledge such power structures, thereby weakening them or even bringing them down.

Psychoanalytic knowledge about people's attitudes toward truth can be helpful in analyzing the forms of ignorance in postindustrial society. Given the power of genetics, forensics, and big data, it is important to look at how people take in this new knowledge and how these sciences are creating both new beliefs in truth and new forms of ignorance.

Chapter 1 asks how our perception of ignorance has changed in contemporary Western society and why the so-called knowledge economy is actually an ignorance economy. To understand how people embrace ignorance and denial in times of crisis, it is useful to look at how these two strategies have been adopted by those who have experienced war. Chapter 2 looks at ignorance and denial among refugees who fled violence during the war in Bosnia and Herzegovina between 1992 and 1995. Many of those people who lost loved ones hope that finding their remains with the aid of DNA will help them to come to terms with their trauma. Developments in genetics, neuroscience, and big data have also led to a belief in the power of DNA more generally and given some the sense that it is possible to come close to the secret of subjectivity itself. But what do we gain by trying to "see" inside the body and by trying to predict and prevent future illnesses with the help of genetic tests? Chapter 3 looks at the fantasies that people create around genes, how they rethink family heritage when they get tested for genetic diseases, and what new anxieties, shame, sorrow, and guilt people suffer from when they try to make sense of their genetic blueprint.

Where traumatic knowledge affects an individual's well-being, ignorance often goes hand in hand with denial. Chapter 4 describes how this operates in relation to health more broadly. In these times of informed consent, people are expected to be fully informed about their illnesses, the range of available medical procedures, and their risks. But people often choose to close their eyes when they face life-threatening issues.

With new types of knowledge about people, forming romantic relationships is increasingly difficult. In order to be attractive to others, people are often advised to appear to be indifferent toward a potential object of affection. Chapter 5 goes on to examine how ignorance works on the intersubjective level, especially in cases of love and hate.

In today's highly individualized society, many people feel that they have been overlooked by others and ignored by society. Some, like the online movement of incels, seek visibility through misogynist writings on the internet, and sometimes with actual physical attacks on innocent people. Chapter 6 explores how the feeling that one has been ignored can be linked to a neoliberal ideology of success and its often "macho" imagery. This ideology has paradoxically contributed to the inadequacy, anxiety, and guilt that people now feel.

In the age of algorithms, big data is changing the way we think about ourselves. Ignorance, however, plays an important role in the way data is collected and used. As in the field of medicine, so in the domain of big data, informed consent obfuscates the mechanisms of power and thus maintains them and contributes to a further increase in ignorance. Chapter 7 reflects on the ideology of self-improvement, which has contributed to an increase in mobile phone applications and various wearable devices with the help of which people hope to change their habits and become more productive while ignoring the fact that these devices are collecting data about them. Those who control society today, be it politically, socially, or commercially, very much rely on the analysis, manipulation, and control of people's behavior with the help of the data collected about them, which is why the opaque world of big data presents an important element in the relationship between power and ignorance.

In times driven by the new fantasies formed around the presumed "truth" about ourselves (fueled by the fascination with genes, brains, and big data) and by the emergence of fake news, which makes it hard to discern where information is coming from and how accurate it is, it is not surprising that ignorance is on the rise. In some cases, this might actually have a positive effect, since it allows people to distance themselves from the dominant ideology and possibly engage in new forms of reflection. However, it is equally important to discern how the mechanisms of power themselves rely on keeping people in the dark about the way they operate.

1

The Many Faces
of Ignorance

THERE ARE TWO WAYS of thinking about ignorance. One meaning of the term relates to the lack of knowledge, or the lack of desire to know, while the second meaning concerns relationships; for example, we choose to ignore or refuse to notice a certain behavior or person. However, there is a crucial difference between the act of ignoring something and the state of being genuinely ignorant of it, even though they can appear to be very similar, even identical. To ignore something means to deny either its importance or its very existence; it also means to overlook it. In contrast, to be in ignorance of something involves a lack of awareness of its actual or even possible presence or meaning in the universe. The difference between the act of ignoring and the state of being ignorant implies the moralistic distinction between the state of responsibility and the state of innocence. Ignoring something that we are actually aware of involves striving to regain the state of bliss that "original" ignorance once provided.

"Ignorance" as a term is frequently used in a negative context and is often something that we accuse others of indulging in.

However, ignorance and ignoring play a crucial role in our daily lives, especially the ways we forge relationships. Without ignorance, love would not exist. Child rearing is full of situations in which a parent will pay complete attention to a child and then studiously ignore him or her. The best way to deal with a toddler's tantrum is often to ignore the child or adopt a "time out" strategy. And what is a "time out," if not a spell in which young children are obliged to accept their parents' ignoring them? Sleeping, too, is essentially linked to ignorance, since insomnia often results from a failure to absorb and dispel daily events and the emotions that they arouse in us.

Strategic ignoring is promoted in schools as well—teachers advise pupils to ignore troublemakers and to pay no attention to their provocations. They will also, at times, ignore the warning signals about personal or family problems that a particularly disruptive pupil's behavior sends. Teachers may sometimes rely on a further distinction between modes of ignoring: to ignore misbehavior when it is a warning of something else being wrong can mean that you heed the warning but decide to disregard it; or it can mean that you genuinely fail to understand it as a warning.

In dating, ignoring flaws can be a way to keep desire alive. When we are designing or making something, we are told to ignore what others are doing so that we can avoid comparing our work with theirs. In our daily lives, we often feign ignorance out of respect for a social norm or one of the "unwritten rules" on which personal relationships are based. Suppose that someone we respect has said something inappropriate or is wearing something we find odd or distasteful. Out of politeness, we might not say anything and might choose to willfully ignore his or her mistake.

Money matters frequently oblige us to blur the lines between genuine and feigned ignorance. At work, employees' salaries are kept secret from each other, and frank discussions about income are taboo in many workplaces—although the holidays, cars, and clothes colleagues can afford often give a good sense of their earnings. At home, some people refuse to share the details of their bank accounts with their spouses, and, more generally, a marriage can be a working example of the delicate but essential distinction between not knowing and not acknowledging, when it comes to one's significant other.

If the capacity to ignore is an essential part of intimate and social relations, the lack of this capacity is often deeply problematic in other areas of our lives. Perceiving and comprehending the world around us necessarily involves deciding what is important to our needs and goals and what is not. People who cannot do this can become incapacitated. A woman with one of the highest IQs ever measured in the United States has explained that she was not able to enjoy a successful career because she simply cannot ignore irrelevant information. She can memorize huge amounts of indiscriminate data, but she cannot judge what is and is not relevant in a given situation. Career-wise, this woman's progress was blocked because she was unable to choose to work or specialize in a profession or field of knowledge. She knows about an enormous variety of subjects, but she lacks the mental "filter" most of us take for granted in deciding what we need and don't need to know.[1]

Ignorance as Protective Stupidity

Confucius pointed out that real knowledge pertains to knowing the extent of one's ignorance. In a similar vein Thomas Jefferson said, "He who knows, knows how little he knows." According to Benjamin Franklin's proverb, "Being ignorant is not so much a shame, as being unwilling to learn." In former socialist countries, such as the Soviet Union and Yugoslavia, political leaders admonished pupils that they needed to study hard. Both Vladimir Lenin and Josip Broz Tito were known for finishing their speeches to students with the slogan, "You have to learn, learn, learn." By contrast, some world leaders today seem to take pride in how little they know. Donald Trump has turned ignorance into a virtue. Many of those who voted for him identified with his apparent lack of knowledge and his lack of shame about his ignorance, which they felt gave him an authenticity that contrasted with the artificiality of many other politicians and technocrats.

Ignorance has also been studied in conjunction with denial. In his book *Denial*, Richard S. Tedlow exposes important cases of denial in business organizations and shows how large corporations profit from them.[2] For Tedlow, denial is a disease that needs to be fought against every single day: "It is a moving target. There is no cure."[3] He takes the example of British Petroleum (BP): In 2010, when an oil spill in the Gulf of Mexico was caused by BP's deepwater drilling, the corporation refused to acknowledge the ecological consequences of this disaster. Tedlow sets out three scenarios to explain the corporation's response. First, it might have been that the company really did not know how grave the situation was. Second, it was possible that officials lower in the corporate hierarchy knew what was happening but were afraid to tell their bosses. And third, it might have been that everyone from top to bottom knew what had happened but decided to close their eyes to the horrible truth. "They saw but they didn't see. They knew but they didn't know. They were protectively stupid."[4]

What does it mean to be protectively stupid? This term was introduced by George Orwell, who in his dystopian novel *1984* presents it as the strategy of "crimestop." Orwell declares it to be "the faculty of stopping short, as though by instinct, at the threshold of any dangerous thought."[5] It includes the more obvious powers of "not grasping analogies, of failing to perceive logical errors, of misunderstanding the simplest arguments" if they are inimical to the powers that be. The Orwellian power is also "bored or repelled by any train of thought which is capable of leading in a heretical direction."[6]

The dean of a Slovenian university used material from a student's diploma paper (without the student's permission) in a report he was paid to write for a commercial enterprise. When he was accused of plagiarism, the representatives of the university engaged in protective stupidity. They claimed that the professor's unauthorized use of his student's work was not such a big deal, for three reasons. First, they claimed that a mentor is like a coauthor of the diploma paper; second, they noted that the student's name was mentioned in a footnote to the professor's commercial report; and third, they pointed out that the professor had signed a contract with the company concerned as an individual and had not provided expert assistance in the name of the university. Instead of simply acknowledging that the professor had presented someone else's work as his own, the university's representatives tried to redefine what really counts as plagiarism. Given the university's strident warnings to students not to plagiarize—and the dire consequences for doing so—it was deeply disturbing when the authorities not only defended one of their highest-ranking professors in such a case but also refused to accept how the rest of the world defines plagiarism. The scandal was soon ignored and the professor never faced any consequences for his action.

In their everyday lives, people often benefit from various forms of protective stupidity or deliberate ignorance. When my friend's partner was dying, she wanted people at dinner parties to ignore the fact that she was going through such a horrible experience. She even explicitly asked visitors not to make her talk about her partner's illness. For her, a few hours of "normal" conversation, in which those present passed over the realities of terminal illness, provided essential relief. It was not that my friend denied what was going on; she simply found comfort and emotional rest in a collective silence on the subject that dominated most of her life during this period. Another couple introduced a similar self-protective embargo when they had to face a fatal illness. One Friday afternoon they decided to start "a disease-free weekend." Although one of the partners was terminally ill and the couple's weekdays were consumed with visits to the doctors, once the weekend began, they agreed not to talk about the condition and pretend that things were normal.

Self-deception, ignorance, and turning a blind eye can also be incredibly useful in our private lives even outside these extraordinary circumstances. Sociologists investigating marital happiness discovered that married people who only see the good and positive traits of their partners were much happier than those who take a more "realistic" view of their spouses.

How is ignorance linked to self-deception? Leonardo da Vinci observed that the greatest deception that people suffer from is their own opinions. Upton Sinclair added that it is difficult to make a man understand something when his salary depends on not understanding it. As Henrik Ibsen reminds us in *The Wild Duck*, if we deprive the average man of his lies, we may also take away his happiness.[7] Sociologists and psychologists who have studied self-deception have observed that people like to think they are self-aware and realistic about themselves, but how accurate is such self-knowledge?[8] In the early 1990s, research on self-deception in academia found out that an improbable 94 percent of American university professors thought that they were better at their jobs than their colleagues. A similar study among high school seniors found that a majority of students thought that they were above average in their ability to get along with others. Of those questioned, 25 percent thought that they were in the top 1 percent.[9]

Knowledge and the Lack of It

How often do we hear people admit that they do not know something? When was the last time a high-ranking politician acknowledged that he or she did not know all the possibly negative outcomes of a policy being promoted? Or that a doctor admitted that he or she did not know how a particular drug might affect the patient?

A number of authors have tried to draw up a taxonomy of ignorance. Ann Kerwin, for example, distinguishes six domains where ignorance is at work:

1. All the things we know we don't know (known unknowns);
2. The things we don't know we don't know (unknown unknowns);
3. The things we think we know but don't (errors);
4. The things we don't know we know (tacit knowns);
5. Taboos ("forbidden" knowledge);
6. Denials.[10]

Nancy Tuana offers a more concise four domains of ignorance:

1. Knowing that we do not know, yet do not care to know;
2. Not even knowing that we do not know;
3. Not knowing because (privileged) others do not want us to know;
4. Willful ignorance.[11]

In some early philosophical writings, ignorance has a certain mystique. The medieval theologian Nicolaus de Cusa is known for his *De Docta Ignorantia*, in which he studied the relation between knowing and not knowing (unknowing).[12] Cusa promoted what he called "learned ignorance"—a knowing state of not knowing. His idea was that we desire to acknowledge what we do not know. But for Cusa, the ultimate truth pertains to the fact that the essence of things, or the truth of beings, cannot ever be fully understood. Therefore, with regard to truth, "we cannot know anything but this: that we know it as incomprehensible in its fullness."[13]

According to Cusa, this recognition is not the end but rather the beginning of genuine understanding. The more deeply we understand our ignorance (or nonunderstanding), "the closer we approach the truth." Put differently, "The more a person knows his or her un-knowing," the more learned he or she is. Hence, just as God's being cannot be entirely fathomed, so too "the essence of all things in their depths remains shielded from our cognition," leaving us in a state of inquiring ignorance.[14]

Today, these words of Cusa seem to be forgotten. The desire to define human beings in terms of biology has recently encouraged efforts to find the "truth" of individual character or subjectivity in genes or in brain cells. This desire to ground the truth of the human psyche in the body paradoxically opens new avenues of ignorance, but not in the "learned" form advocated by Cusa.

Psychoanalysis and Ignorance

From the time of its first practitioners, psychoanalysis has been interested in ignorance. Psychoanalytic theory has also focused on the power of negation and denial, which are both linked to repression. When people "repress" a thought, an image, or a memory, they put it out of their conscious minds. The thought, image, or memory is forgotten beyond recall, because conscious thought cannot bear to know it. A person in analysis, however, who resorts to negation or denial may be doing so because repression is losing its power and the repressed thought is trying to resurface.

Freud advised his clinical colleagues that whenever patients use the negative form, "I'm not," "I didn't," or "This is not so," the analyst needs to pay attention to what comes next, since negation may end up being affirmation, and the patient may start revealing something that has been repressed.

An example of this was when one of Freud's patients was describing a dream and all of a sudden he said, "The woman in my dream is not my mother." The sentence was surprising, since nothing had implied that the woman in the man's dream was his mother. With this negation, the patient found a way to reveal a preoccupation by denying it. As Freud explained, negation becomes a way of making cognizant what is repressed because it gives the repressed idea a verbal existence. Under cover of the patient's "not," the patient's mother entered the scene.[15]

Through negation, a hidden truth can make itself heard, which is to say that negation is the first sign of someone recognizing that something has been repressed, without yet accepting it, which explains the resort to denial. For Freud, denial thus indicates the uncompleted task of recovering repressed content from the unconscious mind while also acting as a weaker deputy for repression. It is, however, important to distinguish between denying and lying. While a conscious lie is an act of intentional deception, denial is an act of unintentional resistance.[16]

In short, when we deny something, we inadvertently reveal exactly what we want to hide. As a result, denial entails the widening of a crack or fault line, where a thought that we were previously not conscious of suddenly emerges. For this reason, somewhat paradoxically, Freud linked negation to the idea of freedom. He pointed out that because denial enables something to emerge that is linked to a repressed memory or feeling, we can finally start working on the significance of the repressed thought. It is, however, also possible that we will resort to new forms of repression.

Post-Freudians also saw the value of denial, and many of them started thinking about the way an individual's denials may be linked to a broader social setting. Otto Fenichel pointed out that a person who denies something often needs to bolster the power of his or her negative declarations with the help of some mythical belief or a simple lie. For example, liars or people who distort particular facts need others to believe in their statements, and it is via this corruption of the record that they themselves enforce their own belief in the lies they tell.[17]

Psychoanalysts are alert not only to the direct negations in denial but also to other words that people use to try to convince their interlocutors that something is not important. Freud pointed out that "only" often plays a particular role in such circumstances. For example, a patient might say, "It is only a dream." A psychoanalyst who hears these words may try to ask why the person seems to play down the importance of the dream that he or she has nonetheless brought up in the session.

Sandor S. Feldman further explored the way denial is often accompanied by certain words or mannerisms. To deny the importance of what we are about to utter, we might start with an off-handed remark, such as "By the way," or "Before I forget." And sometimes we try to mask our dishonesty with insistent phrases like "honestly," "believe me," "frankly," or "to tell the truth." Further ploys to cover up negative feelings include "I wasn't being serious," "I didn't mean to hurt you," or "It was just a joke."[18]

In psychoanalysis, the relationship between analyst and analysand functions with a particular kind of ignorance at its core. Transference, which is an essential element of the analytic relationship, is an emotional bond not dissimilar to love. Before even making the first appointment, the analysand presupposes that the analyst possesses certain knowledge; or as Jacques Lacan would say, the analyst is already the "subject who is supposed to know." Even an analyst with decades of experience can never know what caused the analysand to make an appointment, what unconscious fantasies may be causing trouble or easing pain, and the person's desires or drives. Analysts not only need to refuse to bask in the sun of knowledge, they also need to ignore analysands' attempts to present themselves as objects of love. It is well known that transference in the analytic setting provokes feelings of love for the analyst on the side of the analysand and that these feelings often emerge when the analysand does not want to go any further in exploring unconscious desires or drives.

Lacan's Passion for Ignorance

In the 1950s, the psychoanalyst and theorist Jacques Lacan attended a series of lectures by Paul Demiéville, one of the foremost French scholars of Buddhism. At the same time, the Sorbonne was hosting a renowned Buddhist monk, Walpola Rahula, who became known for his popular introduction to Buddhism, *What the Buddha Taught*. While it is not clear whether Lacan attended Rahula's lectures, it is not surprising that after his interest in Buddhism developed, he began talking about the importance of ignorance in psychoanalytic practice.

In his teaching, Rahula argued that a follower of Buddhism must strive to see clearly and thus be rid of doubt. If doubt is necessary, it must be understood that progress is only possible when one overcomes doubt, perplexity, and wavering and comes close to truth. In this context, ignorance, along with false ideas, is one of the roots of all evil.

Zen Buddhism, however, takes a slightly different approach to ignorance and considers the main problem to be ignorance of ignorance. Here: "Ignorance in itself is no evil, nor is it a source of evil, but when we are ignorant of ignorance, of what it means in our life, then there takes place an unending concatenation of evils."[19]

One can imagine that Lacan found the Buddhist's view of ignorance useful in developing his ideas on psychoanalytic theory and practice primarily because Buddhism does not try to link ignorance simplistically with cognition, but rather with a deeper understanding of the unknown. As Zen Buddhists say, "When we think we know something, there is something we do not know. The unknown is always behind the known, and we fail to get at this unknown knower, who is indeed the inevitable and necessary companion to every act of cognition."[20]

Buddha himself was puzzled by this and was not able to get over ignorance until he transcended the dualism of knower and known. However, this transcendence was not an act of cognition but rather a spiritual awakening. It was self-realization that happened beyond simple cognition. As such, this awakening lay outside the scope of logical reason. While psychoanalysis does not speak about awakening, it nonetheless does say a lot about gaining access to the unknown in its own way. The analyst needs to allow the analysand's speech to proceed in the name of the "passion for ignorance," as Lacan said, without preestablished knowledge and thus without prejudice.

Psychoanalysis has in a variety of ways distinguished between ignorance as it is expressed in different states, such as neurosis, psychosis, and perversion. Freud pointed out that neurosis, in contrast to psychosis, does not disavow reality but only ignores it. Post-Freudian psychoanalysts later looked at how neurotics' unwillingness to recognize reality often fails. Milton Horowitz, for example, analyzed the power of intrusions. After major stressful events, a person might find different strategies with which to deny the emotional impact of the trauma, but then unbidden ideas and surges of seemingly unwarranted feeling might emerge as intrusions, which prevent the person from continuing to ignoring the trauma.[21]

Ignorance and Social Relationships

People often use denial and ignorance as useful strategies to deal with an inconvenient truth that does not fit their perception of reality or as tools to create a fantasy scenario that makes reality more pleasant and easier to bear. These strategies can also be used to keep social relationships intact.

Anthropologist Mark Hobart claims that the growth of knowledge entails a growth of ignorance, but that the nature of this ignorance differs in degree and kind according to the presuppositions of different kinds of knowledge. He takes as an example traditional communities in Senegal, in which people are divided according to their mastery of different crafts. People who by chance know a particular craft but are not part of the group that officially masters it need to pretend that they actually do not possess the skills necessary for that craft. For example, a person who is not from the group of weavers but knows how to weave needs to hide his or her knowledge when in the company of weavers.[22]

Such strategies employ ignorance to keep the relationships between different groups intact. The social significance of secrecy here is that it allows relations between noncraftsmen and artisans to continue in such a way that the status of particular groups is recognized and maintained. In communities where craft occupations are perceived to be hereditary, the fact that people outside a particular group hide their knowledge allows for the continuation of status from generation to generation.[23]

Hobart points out that this use of secrecy develops around a particular cultural politics of denial. In many traditional societies, witchcraft is treated similarly, since such practices and skill in the arts they involve cannot be acknowledged publicly by individuals. Keeping knowledge secret can function as a way of keeping a social hierarchy in place; similarly, not exposing a lie or violence may help to keep power structures intact. All around the world, patriarchal societies systemically ignore violence against women. With the "me too" movement, some small but significant changes have begun with people no longer as willing to tolerate the willful disregard of sexual harassment and sexual aggression against women in the developed world. And with media exposure of violence against women, changes have also started happening in the developing world. American journalist Ellen Barry described how in a small Indian village people witnessed a wife being brutally murdered by her husband. Everyone, however, ignored the crime; official documents stated that the woman died as a result of a fall. The journalist was surprised when she met many witnesses who described how this crime had occurred and was shocked when even the husband admitted to her that he had killed his wife. How was it, then, that the official records stated a blatant lie about this crime? And why, although everyone in the village knew the truth, did no one do anything to expose it? The journalist discovered that the power structure in the village relied on an intricate caste hierarchy, and that if a member of a particular caste had been convicted of murder, this could have cost the politician in power a substantial loss of votes at the next election. The murderer's family bribed the police so they did not investigate the crime. In addition, the powerful village chief spent hours convincing the victim's mother not to press charges. The perpetrator soon found a new young wife who enjoyed wearing the previous wife's jewelry and was not bothered about the way her predecessor had died. Although everyone knew the truth about the crime, they collectively ignored it. This strategy helped the village chief to win the next election, and the hierarchical relationships in the village remained intact.[24] However, when the story was published in the *New York Times*, things suddenly changed. The local police arrested the murderer and he was charged for his crime.[25]

Collective forms of ignorance are also widespread in the developed world. Charles Mills has done extensive research on "white ignorance" as an example of systemic group-based miscognition that has subordinated the nonwhite population over the past few hundred years. The white population has been able to keep its supremacy with the help of white normativity, white narratives that dominate in the society, as well as various forms of social amnesia. Through these strategies, white ignorance allows the continuation of the systemic inequality of the nonwhite population, as well as disregard for racist language and practices.[26]

The Ikeaization of Society

At a time when seemingly unlimited information is available online, it is hard to admit to a lack of knowledge because everyone assumes that with the help of search engines such as Google, there is no excuse for not knowing anything. As a result, everyone is supposed to be master of everything.

This has led in the last decade to what I and others have called the "Ikeaization" of society.[27] Changes in the organization of work have led to a push for knowledge that leaves no space for ignorance. A "do-it-yourself" ideology has permeated every corner of people's lives. As individuals we are expected to learn how to master a huge number of things in our lives: from organizing a holiday, putting together Ikea furniture, and installing new software on one's phone, to diagnosing our own illnesses and finding the best treatment. All involve different levels of knowledge and skill, but the potential availability of information online has created the impression that it is entirely up to us to find answers to our questions, to be experts at everything.

The ideal of the self-made man or woman, on which modern capitalism has relied from its earliest days, has slowly turned into an ideal of self-learning that makes it impossible to admit to not knowing. The downside of the Ikeaization of society is the reluctance to admit one's lack of knowledge. You only need to look on social media to see that people feel confident commenting on things whether they have expertise in the subject under discussion or not.

With the Ikeaization of society, there has also been a change in our relationship to authority. The backlash against experts in the last few years is perhaps not surprising in a world where everyone is an amateur expert and there is increasing skepticism and mistrust of professional expertise. The key factor that has contributed to the erosion of belief in experts is their unwillingness to admit to a lack of knowledge or when something goes wrong—think economists and the financial crisis. And as experiments in social psychology have shown, sometimes having more information gives us the illusion of knowing without understanding.[28]

People who acquire a lot of information on a particular topic may not remember it all or know how to use it. However, they often think they can, which is why their confidence increases. In addition, people are often reluctant to admit that they do not know the answer to a question in their own field of expertise. This overconfidence also affects so-called hindsight bias—the illusion that we knew something all along.

If politicians in the past liked to utter wise words about the necessity of knowing the limits of one's knowledge, today's powerful elites like to show their solidarity with ordinary people through shared ignorance. Power has always relied on people being unwilling to expose the truth—everyone knows the story of the emperor's new clothes. What has changed today is that people are united not in closing their eyes to the truth but rather by their ignorance of what the truth is.

Ignorance, however, is not a simple absence, a lack of knowing. It also has an effect on how knowledge is conceived by a given group or an entire society. The nature of ignorance also depends on the way that a society deals with the consequences of a lack of knowledge: Is it a source of shame or disempowerment, or does it help to define the things an individual does know about, and thus his or her role in society? Alternatively, if knowledge, any knowledge, provides a sense of certainty about things and has a reassuring effect regarding our place in the world, ignorance, by contrast, can suggest uncertainty and a discomfort about the world. If knowledge is believed to be indiscriminately available to all, regardless of education, experience, or natural proficiency, a state of ignorance is all the more degrading.

Ignorance in a Knowledge Economy

We often hear negative statements about the increase of ignorance related to "tunnel vision" and "internet bubbles"—and less often about the "productive" role that ignorance plays in discovering new knowledge. Stuart Firestein, in his book *Ignorance*, shares his experience of teaching a course on ignorance at Columbia University. He asked a number of scientists to confess how essential ignorance is to their work. For Firestein, ignorance was related to necessary gaps in knowledge, an engine that pushes science to acknowledge these gaps, and also something that allows a scientist to continue being self-critical.[29]

In medicine, when doctors lack knowledge, a small act of humility can save a patient's life. A Slovenian professor was known for giving medical students negative points if they wrote what they knew was a manifestly wrong answer in an exam. The student who did not know the answer was encouraged to leave an empty space on the exam sheet, rather than trying to guess the correct answer. The professor justified his approach by saying it was essential that students learn the danger of guessing. The university, however, disagreed with the professor's reasoning and he was ordered to change his grading practice.

Experts' acknowledgment of their ignorance benefits everyone. Nevertheless, there are obstacles in our supposedly "knowledge-based" economy that structurally prevent scientists from learning more. One example is that of scientific journals, which are designed specifically to spread knowledge.

While scientists eagerly engage in the task of writing articles for distinguished journals (and also do the unpaid work of peer-reviewing articles by others), access to materials, once published, can be difficult to secure and often prohibitively expensive. In recent decades some scientific publishers have created an intricate business machine that demands institutions pay extremely high subscriptions for their publications. A paradox has thus emerged that research, which is often government funded, is only available at high cost to libraries, which in turn have to be subsidized by governments in order to be able to pay the subscriptions. For an individual unable to gain access to these libraries, vast amounts of new knowledge are off-limits. Corporate realities are thus making ignorance part of scientific endeavors in a way different from the one Firestein identifies. Ignorance here is linked not to essential gaps in knowledge but instead to structural economic mechanisms, which limit access to knowledge in the interest of profit.

When we hear the term "knowledge-based economy," our first impression is often that the new technologies on which this economy relies contribute to an increase of what is known. Scholars in the domain of management studies have, however, pointed out that the "knowledge economy" should rather be called an "ignorance economy," since it relies heavily on the creation and strategic exploitation of gaps in knowledge. Joanne Roberts and John Armitage point out that "the most important mechanism of the knowledge economy is not necessarily its greater dependence on intellectual abilities, but its greater determination to inhibit such intellectual capabilities."[30]

On the one hand, the knowledge economy very much relies on the way knowledge is restricted, patented, packaged, and compartmentalized. On the other hand, the sophisticated technologies that the knowledge economy exploits make it difficult for people to understand how these technologies work. If we take the example of large internet search engines such as Google, consumers have no clue how the companies' crucial algorithms work, what data is being collected from their searches, or to whom it is sold. And while search engines are of great help to people accessing information, users rarely need to engage in deep thinking about what they learn, since the answers to most questions are just a click away.

The knowledge economy relies on sophisticated participants who have access to all sorts of data, powerful computers, and complicated software, as well as support from educational and consulting services. Essential to these structures are legal mechanisms that protect access to and the use of knowledge by means of trademarks, copyrights, and patents. Familiarity with these intricate, often inaccessible and secretive mechanisms is required to participate in this economy. Roberts and Armitage are right to emphasize that the knowledge economy is actually rooted in the production, distribution, and consumption of ignorance. Yet as Robert N. Proctor has shown in his study of the tobacco industry, the traditional economy has in its own way promoted ignorance in order to increase its profits, whatever the costs to the consumer.[31]

In our private lives, we often have the impression that we can gain access to large amounts of knowledge with the help of new technology, while we pay less attention to how our attention has been affected by using it. The internet has opened vast new possibilities for acquiring information; but it has also reduced our ability to endure the anxiety that comes from lack of understanding.

I remember how, as a first-year undergraduate student, I embarked on the task of studying Kant's *Critique of Pure Reason*. I dived directly into this difficult text. After reading the first twenty pages, I had to admit that I did not understand the main points of Kant's argument. Going through the material was a strenuous exercise in dealing with my lack of knowledge. It was only through persistence—reading the text over and over again, finding background texts that explained the argument, and making comprehensive notes—that I survived that exam. From this experience, I learned a valuable lesson: when learning something new, we need to endure our anxiety about the unknown. For example, when we read a novel in a language that we have not fully mastered, it is more beneficial to accept not fully understanding every word than constantly stopping to check the dictionary. Reading Kant, however, requires higher tolerance for anxiety, since writing like this challenges not only *what* you *know* but also *how* you *think*.

Our attitude toward such anxiety has changed as a consequence of new technology. As soon as anxiety about an unknown kicks in, we have the option of alleviating it. When we do not understand a word in the text, we can easily look it up in an online dictionary. While this kind of quick fix is helpful, it often leads us to spend much more time online than we originally intended, and we are easily distracted from our original task. Not surprisingly, a whole industry has now arisen dedicated to inventing new apps and other devices to help us ignore what is available online. Social media and a constant stream of information have opened up a new market for "ignorance tools"—ranging from app blockers and time-organizing devices to various self-monitoring plans that are supposed to make us more productive and less prone to online distractions. The paradox, however, is that these devices often collect data about the person using them, so while users may be working hard to ignore distractions, the corporations providing them with the tools to do so are definitely not ignoring them.

2

Empty Graves

IGNORANCE, FORGETTING, AND DENIAL IN WAR

WHEN I WAS A LITTLE GIRL growing up in the former Yugo-slavia, we often had to write essays about what our grandparents did during World War II. We were supposed to ask our parents or grandparents (if they were still alive) to recount their heroic acts as partisan soldiers or at the very least supporters of the partisan cause. My parents had only one story. Year after year I wrote out the fable of my deceased maternal grandfather, who owned a bakery in Slovenj Gradec, a small town near the Aus-trian border. One day a wounded partisan fighter sought shelter in my grandfather's bakery. He begged my grandfather to help him get out of town, which meant passing through a German checkpoint. My grandfather had a permit to make deliveries to neighboring villages so he decided to hide the partisan in his van under a pile of bread, risking his own life but in the process saving that of the partisan. For decades after, this heroic story allowed me to navigate my way through the ideological maze of socialist education. "What about my other grandfather? Did he also help the partisans?" I asked my parents. "He did his bit in a small way," my father would reply, "but unfortunately he was unwell and died quite young of lung disease."

Near the end of my time at primary school, my father told me the truth about this other grandfather. He did not die of lung disease but was killed by the Communists in 1946.

My father's family was divided between Austria and what became Yugoslavia in 1920, when plebiscites split the region known as Carinthia between the two countries. Some of my paternal relatives settled in Austria, while others lived in Yugoslavia. This was not unusual; many people were bilingual in that part of the country, and the ties between the Yugoslavian and Austrian branches of the family were very strong. After the partisans won the war, however, neighbors who hoped to climb the ladder of the Communist hierarchy denounced men like those in my father's family as possible Nazi collaborators. My grandfather was imprisoned but was released a year later. That was when his real troubles started. The family waited in vain for him to come home, and only after three years did they learn from an acquaintance with good connections to the Communist Party the reason for his disappearance. When released from prison, my grandfather was offered the choice of staying in Yugoslavia or being transported to Austria; he chose Austria, hoping that with the help of his relatives he would have an easier life there. He expected his wife and three children to join him later. It proved a fatal decision. People who chose to go to Austria were bused to the Yugoslavian border (which after the war was controlled by the Allied forces), but for some reason the Allies had decided without warning to close the border that day, so they were not allowed to cross and were put back on the bus. Instead of being taken home, however, they were driven into the woods in the nearby hills and killed. Someone in the higher echelons of the Communist Party had issued the order that people who were unwilling to help build the country's Communist future should be liquidated. When my father told me this story, we were still living under the Communist regime, and so we knew to keep quiet about such matters. I continued writing the one heroic story of our mother's father, the baker, in school assignments, and the remains of my father's father have never been found. Bones continue to be dug up in the Pohorje woods in northern Slovenia. But these deaths and crimes have no closure.

For the larger part of my childhood, my grandfather's death was ignored. Although it was not publicly spoken about, it was not repressed, as my parents did eventually tell me, but it was revealed not as a truth that had been denied or locked away but rather as a topic that was simply never discussed.

Knowledge like this may be ignored or kept secret, but its emotional impact can be inadvertently transmitted across generations. The story of my grandfather made me wonder about the nature of choice in some surprising ways. My own personal decisions became hard to make; as if making a wrong choice over an ordinary question were a matter of life and death. Choosing where to live became impossible, which is why I have loved working in a number of countries and have avoided deciding on one in particular. At a certain point in my life, I realized that my dilemmas about choice were related to my grandfather. Since learning how he died, I have asked myself why he made the choice he did. I have wondered whether he was naive to have trusted the authorities. Surely the authorities knew all along that they would kill the people who decided to move across the border? And what if his intuition told him not to trust the authorities, but his desire to escape the Communist regime was too strong? If so, did he know that he was taking a risk but accept the offer of relocation anyway? Could he have made a more informed choice in his situation? Behind all these questions was the feeling that choice had become increasingly linked in my mind with death, as if making a wrong choice would always have deadly consequences.

The Many Shades of Ignorance in War

After what had been known as Yugoslavia was broken up in 1991, Slovenia experienced a brief, ten-day war when it was attacked by the Yugoslav army, which was heavily dominated by the Serbian nationalists. To begin with, most Slovenes were clearly in denial and ignored the reality of the military action by the Yugoslav army on the ground. Wishful thinking predominated and it was commonplace to hear things such as, "It cannot be true that an actual war has started; it is probably just a minor military skirmish. Things will soon be back to normal." But within a few days, people started to get anxious, remembering how unexpected and long previous wars in their country had been. Luckily, the aggressively authoritarian regime led by Slobodan Milošević in Serbia was unable to take full control of the Yugoslav air force, so Slovenia was never actually bombed from the air, but many Slovenes expected air raids and spent large amounts of time in shelters. When the all clear came, they ran to the shops and stockpiled food, as well as any protective gear they could find. I remember discovering old Russian gas masks in a shop, which I dutifully bought without realizing that their date of use was long past.

Anxiety in time of war can be overwhelming. I remember how I and a group of friends decided to limit the time we spent listening to the news and embraced a form of willful ignorance when, for a few hours each day, we collaborated on a book. Our subject was a psychoanalytic interpretation of Hitchcock's films. Watching and analyzing films and talking with friends became a way to keep anxiety at bay in a time of complete social panic.

When the short war in Slovenia ended and a much longer and more brutal conflict gained momentum in neighboring Croatia, it was hard to watch a form of political denial emerging in Bosnia and Herzegovina, where the Yugoslav army, which by that time was under full Serbian control, began stockpiling ever more weapons after making its retreat from Slovenia. For many Bosnians it was unthinkable to believe that a full-blown, long-lasting war could erupt. "We, Bosnians, are true Yugoslavs. We believe in transnationality. We are at the center of Europe," was the credo that enabled the denial of what the Yugoslav military's maneuvers in Bosnia meant. Even the Bosnian president, Alija Izetbegović, said, "Sleep peacefully, everyone, there will not be a war."[1]

When the war started in 1992, large numbers of Bosnian refugees started coming to Slovenia, where they were greeted with much compassion. Many Slovenians strongly identified with the refugees since they still remembered their own short war and felt that they had only just escaped a similar fate. Identifying with someone is also easier when one has the pleasure of admiring one's own sense of charity and compassion. But after a few years, this sense of identification grew less strong as many Slovenes, along with the rest of the world, became much less heedful of the Bosnians who were already living in Slovenia, as well as the new migrants and refugees who came after them.

Knowing and Not Knowing Twenty Years after the War: From Bosnia to St. Louis

When Bosnians commemorated the twentieth anniversary of the genocide in Srebrenica and the end of the war in 1995, I started to ask myself how those who survived dealt with the knowledge that many of their loved ones were buried in mass graves that are still being discovered and exhumed. With my own family history in mind, I wondered how knowing, not knowing, or not acknowledging these terrible truths was playing out in a time when forensic analysis allows victims to be identified. I also wanted to observe what happens after more than twenty years when knowledge of what happened in the past has been made public and when people who fled the war have started to be more fully integrated into new communities. The largest number of Bosnian refugees in the United States live in St. Louis, where there is also a vibrant psychoanalytic community led by Todd Dean, who has been offering pro bono help to refugees for years.[2] I decided to visit St. Louis in 2013 to explore how the refugees were dealing with the past and how they have settled in their new country.

My introduction to St. Louis started with a strange exchange with a taxi driver. When I asked the driver to go to Little Bosnia (a part of St. Louis where a large group of Bosnians live), he became visibly angry and reluctant to take me there. A black man in his early sixties, he had been a soldier who served in the NATO forces stationed in Bosnia. When he retired, he started driving a taxi to supplement his meager pension. In his view, the Bosnian refugees in St. Louis had better lives than he did. He said that the government had abandoned him and that his well-being was lower on the government's list of priorities than that of the refugees. He was especially angry that some refugees had really "made it" in their new country—by establishing lucrative businesses, buying large houses, and getting welfare benefits from the state, they seemed to have had more success than he ever could.

When I got there, however, I discovered that Little Bosnia was far from being a promised land where refugees built new lives at the expense of other US residents. Instead, it was a wasteland, a ghost town, haunted by a long-gone past, a past that was never as ideal as it was remembered.

My first stop in Little Bosnia was a small, decrepit restaurant called Stari Grad (Old Town), which inside looked like a scene from an old Yugoslav movie. There were shabby tables covered with plastic tablecloths, kitschy Christmas decorations on the walls, and the smell of tobacco in the air. All around the place hung neatly framed black-and-white photos of Bosnian towns—the remnants of a life lost forever. No customers were in the restaurant, just an old woman behind the bar who eyed me suspiciously when I asked her where she came from originally. Reluctantly, she told me that she was from the Bosnian town of Prijedor, that many members of her family had perished in the war, and that she had never truly settled in the United States. She still did not speak English well; the restaurant was barely surviving, and she had a strong desire to return one day to Bosnia. However, there was little to go back to—her house had been destroyed and her friends and relatives were less than enthusiastic about keeping in touch with her. They imagined that she had a good life in the United States, which they were envious of, and she was reluctant to tell them the truth.

My next stop in Little Bosnia was the Bosnian soccer club. Here the scene was slightly more upbeat since the local Bosnian soccer team had just won an important diaspora tournament. The place looked like a 1970s socialist canteen, with shabby wooden chairs, green tablecloths, and photos of soccer players and club paraphernalia on the walls. The story of the club manager was similar to that of the woman from the restaurant. He had also escaped from the war and now had nowhere to return to. During the war, as he was running for shelter with his children, his five-year-old daughter suddenly tripped and fell to the floor, and a Bosnian Serb soldier killed her in front of his eyes. He and the rest of his family ended up in camps, while the little girl's body was buried by the Serbs together with other victims of that attack in a nearby graveyard. The horror of the loss of his daughter was made even worse when he learned that later, in order to cover up their crimes, the perpetrators had scattered the remains of the people they had buried in other secret mass graves. He now spent every summer in Bosnia searching for his daughter's remains. A great believer in the power of forensic science, he hoped that with the help of DNA analysis, he would one day be able to find his daughter's bones and finally build a memorial for her, allowing him some form of closure.

People who have experienced terrible loss and suffering often express feelings of guilt for failing to do the right thing before the event occurred. The Bosnian Serb military commander, Ratko Mladić, was one of the key people who was tried for the 1995 genocide that happened in Srebrenica, where more than eight thousand Bosnians were killed.[3] The first person to testify at this trial was Elvedin Pašić, who now lives in St. Louis.[4] As a fourteen-year-old boy, he had witnessed his father being taken away with other men from his village. He and his mother ended up in the concentration camps, and he later learned that his father and the other men had been brutally murdered. Pašić broke down during his testimony, sobbing when he spoke of how he had had the chance to see his father one last time but had decided not to. He still regretted the fact that he had missed that opportunity. The memory of his dead father haunted him even more since he had his own children. When he was asked what he hoped would come out of the Mladić trial, he said that he would like to learn where his father's remains were.

Another Bosnian refugee in St. Louis, Ertana Dzidzović, remembered how at the time of the war, when she was twelve years old, she learned that a friend who had offered to pick some apples for her from a nearby garden in Sarajevo had been killed by enemy fire.[5] Dzidzović and her family fled the country. They too, at some point, settled near other Bosnians in St. Louis. Because of what she witnessed during the war, Dzidzović felt she was radically different from other women her age: "I feel 100 years old because of my experience." Nowadays, however, she rarely talks about her past: "I want to set it aside and keep on living. . . . It's not like I forgot. I don't want to remember."[6]

A strategy of willed nonrecall functions in the same way as the kind of willful ignorance that keeps the past in the past. Yet even when a person does not want to consciously remember a traumatic event, unwanted memories can still disrupt the defenses so carefully built up against it. Many older women in Little Bosnia, for example, have found refuge in work, often working long hours in low-paid manual jobs (as cleaners or in restaurants). They need the money. But for many of these women, work also offers refuge from a painful past: as long as they work hard, memories are less likely to haunt them. But then, if they have an accident or get ill or there is some other unpredictable disruption of their routine, the painful memories return. Suddenly, the defenses built up through relentless activity collapse—and the world they have so carefully constructed starts to crumble.[7] Depression often follows, along with an inability to make sense of what happened.

In a Bosnian butcher's shop in St. Louis, I by chance encountered a man who used to be a truck driver. His life was going well, he was earning a good living, and the war seemed to be behind him—until he had a traffic accident. Although he recovered rather quickly from his physical injuries, the accident unleashed terrible memories that caused him to suffer a total collapse. He ended up in a psychiatric hospital and was never able to work again. When I saw this man, he looked like a shadow of a human being—there was something dead in the way he talked; all the energy seemed to have been sucked from his middle-aged body. In our brief encounter, he also seemed to be afraid that talking about his experience would lead to further damage.

Talking about terrible loss or pain is particularly problematic for people who come from communities where talking openly about things might have unexpected consequences or even be genuinely dangerous if the information were reported to the authorities. For example, in former Communist countries, mental health issues were stigmatized and people who suffered from them were frequently hospitalized, often against their will. Moreover, in patriarchal communities, men were discouraged from showing any signs of vulnerability.

Psychoanalyst Todd Dean told me that in St. Louis Bosnian refugees often went to a psychiatrist or other kind of therapist when they had problems with the law—for example, when they had committed a crime and were afraid they might lose their refugee status.[8] They would start talking about symptoms like nervousness and insomnia, and while at first it might seem as if they were malingering and seeking treatment only to obtain documents that might help them with the state authorities, their sessions provided a way for them to uncover and acknowledge horrifying past experiences.[9]

Dean described the case of Ibro, who complained about his asthma. His symptoms got worse every year around Christmas, so much so that he could not make phone calls to his family in Europe. In analysis, Ibro remembered that the time when he first became physically unable to talk on the phone was a particular moment during the war. Unaware that Bosnian Serbs were building camps in a nearby village, he was shocked when men from his own village were suddenly taken away and did not come back. His wife urged him to hide, assuring him that women and children were usually spared in such circumstances, so he agreed to go into hiding. A few days later when he called home, he learned that his wife and children had been taken to the camps. On hearing this devastating news, he suddenly became unable to use the telephone. After the war Ibro was reunited with his family; they immigrated to the United States, and there he again became incapable of talking on the phone. In addition, he started having moments when he found himself crying uncontrollably.

Ibro thought these problems somehow had a physical cause, and started going to doctors to find out what was wrong with his body. He also claimed that he did not speak English, which is why a translator helped him when he talked to the analyst. However, one day when the translator was unable to come to the session, Ibro had no problem expressing himself in English. Suddenly, the way he talked about his troubles also changed. Instead of searching for a physical cause, Ibro finally allowed himself to deal with his emotions and slowly started to recall and address his memories of the war.

Studies on trauma show that people often repress memories of traumatic experiences in a desperate attempt to go on living. For the person to survive, the knowledge of the horror that has happened often needs to be deflected, hidden, or disconnected from ordinary experiential knowledge.[10] The impossibility of putting a painful experience into words is highlighted in a story told by Ruth Wajnryb in which an adult daughter asks her mother to describe her experiences in a Nazi concentration camp. The mother does not want to talk about it, but when the daughter insists, the mother responds by sending her daughter a letter that consists of four blank pages.[11] While a person may not be able to easily recall painful events from the past and put them into words, this does not mean that these events are forgotten. Jacques Lacan warns that although the traumatic event might be something that the person cannot speak about, it remains "somewhere, spoken . . . by something the subject does not control."[12] As Ibro's case shows, a problem he had with making phone calls to Europe at Christmastime was related to what he could not put into words about his painful experience from the war.[13]

Gilead Nachmani, in his study on trauma and ignorance, has looked at how normal cognitive processes can be disrupted by a sense of helplessness, one of the common elements of trauma.[14] As a consequence, the victim's memory of the traumatic experience can become blurred, partial, or distorted, or disappear altogether. The recollection of trauma becomes impossible, because no matter how much a victim wants to remember it, he or she cannot recall the salient details. Nachmani asks, "Is being informed, becoming more aware, therapeutically desirable? What must a person do to 'reassociate' what has been dissociated?"[15] He concludes that the process of working through the horrifying experience requires the victim to go beyond simply "knowing the trauma"—for example, by listening to others talk about it. The victims have to be able to formulate their painful experience in their own words in such a way that they no longer ignore but are able to recognize the effects it has had on them.

Trauma and New Knowledge

When refugees are haunted by violent experiences from the past, they often find it hard to learn a new language or absorb basic information about their new country.

In St. Louis, lawyers and analysts who work with the refugee population recalled the case of a Somali woman, let us call her Ardo, who fled violence in her homeland almost twenty years ago and ended up as a refugee in the United States. Ardo wanted to settle in her new home but was unable to learn English well enough or memorize trivial facts such as how many states are in the United States or who the first president was, so she had failed the US citizenship test despite many attempts. The lawyers assisting her in her application for citizenship were surprised that this otherwise intelligent woman had failed so many times, and they called a psychoanalyst friend to try to understand why Ardo could not memorize the answers to such simple questions.

At first Ardo gave her psychoanalyst the impression of being a well-adjusted young woman with a strong desire to become an American citizen. There was only one problem with her new homeland—the cold. After arriving in the United States, she ended up in Michigan, where the winters are freezing. She shared a house with other Somali refugees, where her preferred place was in the kitchen, near the stove. Soon, she did not want to leave the spot and stayed in the kitchen all the time. The voices of men whom she heard from other rooms made her anxious, as did the cold weather—only the heat of the stove and the voices of other Somali women could relieve her anxiety, at least temporarily.

Then one day, this young woman was involved in a minor car accident on an icy road. Although the damage was relatively minor and she was not seriously injured, Ardo's world collapsed. She fell into a deep depression and even contemplated suicide. After more than a decade, memories of terrifying events from her time in Somalia started resurfacing. As with the case of the Bosnian truck driver from St. Louis, an insignificant car crash unlocked old memories of violence. But in contrast to the man who had seemed so lifeless when I met him at the butcher shop, Ardo, with the help of extensive therapy, slowly worked through her traumatic past and in time started living a full and productive life. She also passed her citizenship test without problems.

A sudden shock and extensive therapy helped Ardo unblock the memories of trauma that had unconsciously weighed so heavily on her mind that she was unable to think about anything else, including acquiring new knowledge and skills. Her mind was so busy trying to actively ignore what had happened to her that it was ignorant of everything else. Psychoanalyst Julio Granel noticed that in some people an accident helps to give shape to what was previously somehow without shape.[16] Before the accident, a person could be suffering serious anxiety. Then, all of a sudden, the drama of the inner world is replaced by a drama in the outside world—anything from a minor traffic accident to a hurricane. This abrupt intrusion from the outside world demands the person's full attention, and the individual is shocked from his or her anxiety into some kind of choice or action. The British psychoanalyst Wilfred Bion believed that an accident or disaster could provide a way for an individual to seek or even find meaning. Individual developmental changes often occur in moments of violence or chaos. Sometimes a new idea or way of seeing oneself only emerges through the onset of disruptive forces.[17]

Lost Bodies

It is hard enough when people lose a loved one, but it is a cause of great trauma and pain when they do not know where their loved one is buried. In Bosnia, there is an ongoing search for the remains of the victims of the massacres. The Missing Persons Institute of Bosnia and Herzegovina has now identified twenty thousand out of thirty thousand missing persons, and every year people in Bosnia organize burials to reinter exhumed and identified victims.

Red Rubber Boots, a short documentary film by Jasmila Zbanić, shows the journey of a woman who accompanies forensic expert Amor Mašović as he excavates mass graves scattered around Bosnia and Herzegovina.[18] This woman lost two small children in the war, and she hoped that with the help of DNA analysis, she might find their remains. After visiting many gravesites and finding no trace of her lost children, her only hope lay in discovering a pair of red rubber boots that one of her boys was wearing when he was killed. Since plastic does not decompose, she hoped that these boots would show her where her two sons had been buried. In the film, we see her being driven from one mass grave to another. Her face looks frozen. She shows no emotion, but then suddenly, in a rather dispassionate voice, she mentions that she does not dream of her children, unlike other women who have lost their children. These other women meet their children in their dreams and they are happy. But for her, there is no solace to be had either in finding the bodies of her sons or in encountering them in their dreams.[19]

Mašović points out that in some cases, mothers of sons who were killed refused to assist with the DNA analysis because finding a DNA match would give their loss an absolute finality that they were not prepared to deal with. In other cases, investigators could not find a DNA match because the deceased had no surviving relatives.

As Mašović concludes, "The families of the missing are the biggest victims of this war. You have nowhere to mourn." He calls this impossible mourning "a genocide that lasts." It is no longer a crime against the dead, he explains. "This is genocide of the living."[20]

In her work on forensic research in Kosovo, Rachel Cyr warns that progress in forensics "carries with it the very real potential of decentering eyewitness and survival testimony."[21] Physical evidence is often the most powerful weapon against denial that atrocities happened in the first place or that people in charge knew about them.[22] But the belief in forensic science also opens up the fantasy that every found fragment can be identified, if only the proper techniques can be developed. Cyr warns us that forensics opens up the fantasy of finding an ultimate witness— "the one who could see and recover everything."[23]

Cyr also discusses the differences between a tomb, which can retroactively give symbolic meaning to sites though it might very well be physically empty, and a grave, which usually contains a body that can be looked at, analyzed, or counted. An empty tomb can be more than a sign that something is missing from it; it can also serve to mark a loss that no physical evidence can eradicate—a loss that individuals deal with in their own way, a loss that evades words, a loss around which stories can circulate, but a loss that is often linked to silence.

My family decided to create an empty tomb for my grandfather. Twenty years ago, when my grandmother died, the family inscribed his name next to hers on her gravestone, which stood above her burial plot. This inscription transformed her grave into a half-empty tomb full of symbolic meaning.

Denial of Evidence

In the aftermath of large-scale atrocities, another battle often begins over numbers. Holocaust denial and the still-unaccounted-for dead from the Bosnian and Kosovo wars are pressing examples of such struggles to control the past. In the Balkan context, the question of the exact number of victims soon became a battleground in which the two sides continued the conflict, either by scaling down the numbers or by augmenting them, using negation, statistics, and other abstractions.

The International Criminal Tribunal for the Former Yugoslavia was established by the United Nations in 1993 to prosecute war crimes that happened after the collapse of Yugoslavia. During the trials at this tribunal, factual or forensic evidence was presented alongside the narratives of survivors and perpetrators. Simultaneously, however, the perpetrators, especially those living in the Serb-controlled territory in Bosnia and Herzegovina, gathered and presented their own evidence, mostly denying their crimes and presenting themselves as victims.[24] Slobodan Milošević was a master of both numerical revisionism and negation—he even demanded that a BBC journalist, who testified at his trial in The Hague, admit that "he saw nothing" of the alleged mass graves in Kosovo.

Jovana Mihajlović Trbovc has analyzed memories and narratives of victims and perpetrators of ethnic cleansing in Prijedor, the town from which many refugees in St. Louis came from and which is now part of the Serb-controlled territory called Republika Srpska, one of the two political entities of Bosnia and Herzegovina.[25] Officials in the Prijedor Municipality used various strategies to avoid dealing with the fact that between 1992 and 1995 large numbers of local Muslims were placed in camps around the city, where they lived in the most inhumane circumstances and where many women were raped and many people killed. Mihajlović Trbovc observed different forms of denial of these crimes at work in the narratives that were formed about the past. Politicians in the municipality liked to stress that the Serbs were the victims of ethnic cleansing by the Nazis during World War II. To commemorate these losses they established a special memorial day and erected a monument to the victims of Nazi crimes. The next strategy of denial was to claim that the detention camps where the Serbs locked up the Muslims at the time of the Bosnian war actually had nothing to do with ethnic cleansing. They became, in the official town discourse, "provisional collection centres for persons captured in combat or detained on the grounds of the Security Services' operational information."[26] Victims, however, call these camps "the first concentration camp in Europe after World War II" and "a factory of death."[27]

After the Bosnian war, there were almost no non-Serbs living in the area of Prijedor, which is why attempts to formally commemorate the victims started only after 2000 when Bosnian Muslims started returning to the area. Local politicians then found another excuse for not supporting commemoration and the creation of a memorial. Their explanation was that any commemoration of the Bosnian war would prevent multiethnic relationships from being reestablished. They were worried that erecting a monument to the people killed in detention camps would hurt the feelings of the local Serbian population. Another excuse the politicians used was to insist that they would commemorate the losses of the Muslim population but only after a proper monument was built in Sarajevo to commemorate the losses that Serbs suffered there.[28]

At the trials in The Hague, the perpetrators found all kinds of excuses when they were asked to testify in court. When Ratko Mladić was called to the witness stand at the trial of his collaborator, the former psychiatrist Radovan Karadžić, he said that he could not talk because he did not have his dentures. Mladić demanded that his false teeth be brought to the courtroom so that he would be able to speak. When the guards complied with this demand, Mladić, however, did not share his knowledge about what had happened during the war. Instead he started an attack on the members of the judiciary by saying, "I do not recognise this Hague Court, it is NATO's creation, a Satanic court, not a court of justice. . . . It is trying us for protecting our own people from you."[29]

Mladić's lawyer, Branko Lukić, tried to save the situation by claiming that in any event, his elderly client could not be of much help to the court since his recollection of events was shaky as a result of his suffering from a syndrome known as "deception of memory." According to Lukić, this "category of memory disorder" means that "somebody cannot differentiate between truth and fact, because they speak the truth even if they are not doing so."[30] With this confusing explanation of an alleged memory disorder, Lukić tried to help his client avoid having to reveal what had actually happened in the war.

While Slobodan Milošević died in prison in The Hague before his trial came to an end, in 2017 Mladić was found guilty of ten of the eleven charges he was facing, including the genocide at Srebrenica. He was sentenced to life imprisonment. Many relatives of the victims of Mladić's crimes were in attendance when the court pronounced the verdict. Among them was Nedžiba Salihović, a woman who had lost her husband, son, and father in the Srebrenica massacre. In 1995 Salihović had been photographed by Ron Haviv in Tuzla, where she had just arrived with thousands of tormented refugees, mostly women, who came out of the besieged Srebrenica. Haviv's photo depicts Salihović standing behind a UN soldier with a pained expression on her face and her arms spread toward the sky as if asking for help. When, more than twenty years later, Salihović heard the verdict at Mladić's trial, she jumped from her seat, again spreading her arms out wide, but this time screaming for joy that the truth had finally been found and justice had been served.[31]

Some refugees in St. Louis were probably equally overjoyed when they learned that Mladić had been found guilty for his crimes, but for many, not much changed in their lives when his trial ended. For the people of Little Bosnia, the past is not just present in their memories; the way they organize their spaces, their little shops and restaurants, all reminds them of times past. On my last day in St. Louis, I visited a Bosnian grocery store, which was full of produce from the republics of the former Yugoslavia. Slovenian juice and mineral water shared space on the shelves with Croatian fish tins, and Serbian beans sat next to Bosnian coffee and sweets. Behind the counter was a large photo of the late president Josip Broz Tito neatly dressed in a military uniform adorned with decorations. The shop looked like a fairy-tale fantasy space—a harmonious reunion of the former Yugoslav republics represented through their food. The place, however, was deserted, as if the items of food and drink were all that were left of the long-lost past.

3

The Secret in the Body

KNOWLEDGE AND IGNORANCE
ABOUT GENES

IN *THE GENE FOR DOUBT*, the Greek novelist Nikos Panayoto-poulos imagines a society in the near future where scientists have discovered a gene that determines artistic talent.[1] With the help of a simple test, a person can immediately learn whether he or she is genetically "marked" to be a creative artist. As a result, both the art market and the literary world change rapidly. Those visual artists or writers with the creative gene thrive, while those without it slowly fall into oblivion. Many renowned writers initially resist taking the test, but they gradually change their minds as the publishing industry starts to publish only the works of genetically verified artists. The story is different for young artists and writers: if they possess the right gene, no matter what they write gets published by prestigious presses, while established art galleries will only promote those with the artistic gene. The relatives of deceased artists start opening graves in hopes of providing testable evidence that their long-dead grandfather or aunt possessed the gene, thus triggering an increase in the value of their works. The main character of the book is an old writer who refuses to undergo the test, without realizing that he is thus condemning himself to oblivion. He bravely suffers the painful consequences of his decision and starts to write in praise of doubt. On his deathbed, the writer gives in to curiosity and takes the test, but then decides not to look at the results and dies with his doubt intact. The reader learns that the writer did actually carry the desirable gene, but in the meantime his commitment to a life of uncertainty and ignorance has contributed to a reversal of social attitudes, and the gene test slowly loses its power.

This is a fictional account of the power of genetics. In everyday life, however, we often perceive genes as possessing a secret that needs to be discovered to unlock the truth about our bodies and thus predict the future of ourselves and our offspring. Genetics has opened the door to a radical rethinking of subjectivity and fostered new types of fantasies, anxieties, and paranoia.

Might it be better to embrace ignorance when it comes to genetic testing for potential future illnesses? Many who undergo genetic testing have problems dealing with the results: some regret taking the test at all, while others struggle to establish exactly what the results mean in terms of their risk of developing a specific illness in the future, and some go from one test to another, often getting different results from different commercial organizations, failing to find the certainty they seek.

Anxiety about what happens to those test results and who gets to see them is also on the rise. Opportunities for misuse are plentiful—from state surveillance to people being unable to get health insurance or being charged excessively high premiums because they have been identified as having a genetic predisposition to developing a particular medical condition in the future. Likewise, in the field of criminology, there is an abundance of theories surrounding the idea that there might be a genetic pre-disposition to crime—similar to the nineteenth-century notion that some are "born criminal," developed in work of Cesare Lombroso. While some hope that a greater understanding of genetics might lead to less punitive sentencing, others caution that those perceived as genetically predisposed to antisocial behavior will be subjected to new forms of social control. Here, too, the question is what to do with this new knowledge. While an individual might opt to remain ignorant, like the writer in *The Gene for Doubt*, on the societal level it is too late—the genie has already escaped from the bottle. As a result it is impossible to ignore the way genetics affect how we think about ourselves, our relationships, and our work.

I Know Very Well, But . . .

In 2013 I attended a conference in Cambridge in honor of the sixtieth anniversary of the discovery of DNA. This event at-tracted major geneticists, along with a number of entrepreneurs who were hoping to launch new businesses related to genetic research. One of these entrepreneurs had the idea of developing a genetic dating app. He had calculated that it would soon cost very little to get a person's genome decoded and predicted that computer scientists would then be able to link an individual's genetic information to his or her online dating profile. In addi-tion, he imagined that it would be possible to synchronize this information between mobile dating apps in such a way that after the first date, people would be able to get information about the genetically determined illnesses their dating partners, potential mates, and potential children might be likely to de-velop.[2] When I asked this entrepreneur whether people would truly like to—or be entitled to—acquire all this information after no more than a first date, he replied that it would help to avoid wasting time with a person who had "bad" genes.

If, in the past, love was perceived as being essentially "blind" and we fell in love with our eyes and our minds half-closed, in the future it seems there might be a danger that we try to see and know too much. If genetic information becomes widely available and easily interpreted with the help of algorithms and applications on smartphones, all kinds of paranoia and anxiety might be expected to overshadow our romantic encounters.

When people are in the grip of anxiety, ignorance is often, at least temporarily, an efficient defense. However, can one afford to be ignorant of the information from genetic testing? How do we deal with the data presented to us in the results of commercially branded genetic tests? At the same Cambridge conference, anxiety about commercial genetic testing was expressed by a geneticist who rejected such tests on rational and scientific grounds but was still curious about the genetics industry. He decided to send one company a sample of his saliva, intending to make fun of the nonsensical predictions he expected them to offer. When the test results arrived, the scientist was amused to read the estimations of the risk he bore of developing a number of illnesses at some point in the future. His attitude changed, however, when at the end of the message he was offered the option of receiving further information about his genes. This choice made the scientist anxious. Although he did not believe in commercial genetic testing, the possible nature of the information the message claimed to contain disturbed his scientific skepticism.

To regard genetic testing with such anxiety ignores what science tells us about the way genes work. Except for a few illnesses associated with particular genes, most are not transmitted simply through DNA. Epigenetics, the interaction of genes with environmental, social, or cultural factors, also play an important role but are often ignored when people think about the power of genes. As a result, all kinds of fantasies are created around what is supposedly passed down to us from our parents and through us to our children.

I remember that when my son first learned about genetics in primary school, he was upset to discover that some illnesses and conditions—such as myopia—are hereditary. Since he is shortsighted, as am I, he was quite unhappy that I hadn't fixed my faulty gene before I had him. I tried to explain that technology does not yet allow for such interventions. My son finally calmed down when he remembered that half of his genes came from his father and included, in his opinion, some very good ones. When I asked which gene he was particularly pleased about, he responded, "A gene for not having too many friends." At that time, my son often objected that I had too many friends. Genes provided my son with a useful explanation for his dissatisfaction at being dragged to social events when he would rather have stayed home and played alone.

Wrongful Birth: Rationalizing the Unknown

In 2016, three Canadian families filed a "wrongful birth" action against a sperm bank based in Georgia, in the United States, and its Canadian distributor.[3] They alleged that the sperm bank had failed to investigate the background of a particular donor and thus had committed fraud against those who bought his sperm. The families had chosen the donor concerned because he seemed to be "the best of the best." The sperm bank advertised him as having an IQ of 160 and as being an internationally acclaimed drummer working on a PhD in neuroscience engineering who spoke five languages and read four to five books per month. One Canadian family, who was already raising a healthy boy conceived with sperm from this donor, received an email from the agency that accidentally revealed the man's identity. After searching online, the family found out that the donor was actually a convicted felon who had been diagnosed with multiple mental illnesses, including schizophrenia, narcissistic personality disorder, and grandiose delusions. He was not a PhD student with an exceptionally high IQ but actually someone who had taken twenty years to finish his undergraduate degree.

This particular donor's sperm was used to conceive as many as thirty-six children in Canada, the United States, and Great Britain. When the news of the fraud became public, a number of families filed lawsuits. One mother said that her son had not shown any signs of mental illness to date, but she was afraid that his life could turn on a dime at puberty. She pointed out that she had spent four months researching which donor to choose and had chosen this particular company because it claimed that its donors were all from the top 1 percent of the population in terms of health and achievement. This mother and other affected families planned to use any financial compensation they received from the sperm bank to pay for regular testing and treatment if their children showed signs of mental health problems later in life. By 2018, the court in Atlanta had dismissed three lawsuits against the sperm bank, claiming that the law in Georgia does not recognize the term "wrongful birth."[4]

While the sperm bank undoubtedly fraudulently misrepresented the donor, there is also the important question of how the children involved might be affected by the case.[5] If they learned about the circumstances of their conception, they might also learn that while their mothers expected half their genes to have come from a highly intelligent father, they were in fact deceived and the children are actually carrying the genes of someone with a criminal record who is also mentally ill. I have to wonder whether it might have been better for the family who first received the email that revealed the name of the donor to embrace willful ignorance—to resist the temptation to do research on the internet and to embrace the reality that reproduction is essentially linked to the unknown. A woman who conceives a child with a sexual partner should know that it is impossible to predict how the combination of their genes will affect the new human being they create. And someone who conceives with the help of a sperm donor can never be sure that any of the donor's past successes or his qualities will lead to similar outcomes for her child.

The term "wrongful birth" itself could also create a lot of problems for a child who was conceived with the "wrong" sperm or the "wrong" implanted egg. When children go through the phase of questioning whether they were wanted, they often wonder whether their parents wanted to have a child of another sex or with different qualities.

The question "Who am I?"—which often focuses on what significant others (notably parents) desire us to be—continues well into adulthood. Psychoanalysis has dealt extensively with the impossibility of ever getting a satisfying answer to this question. The subject can only interpret the parents' or other people's words and behavior, read between the lines, and in the end create a fantasy answer that will never satisfy. One wonders what kind of fantasies or anxieties might develop in children who learn that they were "wrongly" born. It is quite possible that some might be angry with their parents for searching for the "truth" about the sperm donor, because that truth, for a start, probably changed how the parents regarded their children and affected what they desired or expected from them.

"Wrongly born" children might later start perceiving any psychological hurdle in their lives as a sign of a mental illness or personality trait inherited from the donor's genes; and parents might take any unruliness as a sign of genetically influenced delinquent behavior, beyond their control or responsibility.

The issue of how a child might feel about learning that he or she was born from the "wrong" sperm is also relevant to the case of a white lesbian couple who sued a sperm bank on the grounds that the couple were sent sperm from a black donor instead of the white one they had requested. The couple said that they wanted a donor with genetic traits similar to both of theirs and had picked one after carefully reviewing his history. When one of them got pregnant and they learned about the mix-up, their joy soon turned into a nightmare: "All of the thoughtful planning and care that she [Jennifer] and Amanda had undertaken to control their baby's parentage had been rendered meaningless. In an instant Jennifer's excitement and anticipation of her pregnancy was replaced with anger, disappointment and fear."[6]

After their daughter was born, the couple blamed the sperm bank for an unplanned transracial parent-child relationship, which forced them to move to a place that was more racially and culturally diverse. While they insisted that they loved their daughter, they pointed out in court that they were not equipped to deal with the challenges of raising a child of mixed race. One of the women stressed that she had limited "cultural competency" with African Americans and did not want her daughter to feel stigmatized because of the circumstances of her birth.

When the parents were asked how they thought their daughter might feel about the lawsuit when she was old enough to understand it, they said, "She'll know the lawsuit was about a company that had to make changes and give us compensation so that we can go through counselling and learn how to love each other even more."[7] The court dismissed the case, but the sperm bank partially refunded the parents the cost of the sperm anyway.

Both lawsuits for "wrongful birth" claimed that any money paid out by the sperm bank would be used to provide therapy for the child involved, as if the parents in these cases were expecting something to go wrong with their children. The parents seem to have assumed that by choosing a "perfect" donor with a high IQ or from a specific racial background, they could somehow preset "desirable" biological features in their future children simply by trusting the descriptions in the sperm bank catalogs and the power of genetic selection. But when they had to deal with their anxiety over their children having the "wrong" genes, they seemed to suddenly lose their faith in biology and to hope that therapy would compensate for the harm done by "wrongful birth."

Secrets of the Body

Because science has taught us that genes are so important, some people feel it is vital to "see" or understand their genes. But because so much remains unknown about genes—what they look like or how they work—the picture that we try to develop of our genes owes more to ignorance and the realm of imagination than to the findings of biological science. In other words, such a picture more accurately reflects the state of our individual psyches than it does the latest results from the laboratory.

Despite all that experimental science has taught us, people still tend to understand their bodies in terms of what Aristotle called a "substantial form" (*morphe*).[8] In thinking about the state of their bodies, people believe that their physical condition is dictated and controlled by an underlying form or predefined state. This underlying form, as Aristotle saw it, is thus the "explanatory cause" of the physical state in which people find themselves.

Our genes have now become implicated in this idea of the body's substantial form: in our minds, genes are a big part of the explanatory cause by which we understand who we are. Thinking about genes as a "cause" also affects the way we see our parents and families—from whom we got those genes in the first place. After suffering a stroke, J. Allan Hobson wrote a memoir in which he says that his genes presented him with a particular kind of "Hobson's Choice": the alternative fates he had been allotted genetically were either Alzheimer's on his mother's side of the family or cardiovascular disease on his father's side.[9]

After his stroke, Hobson felt that a little bit of him had died as a result of the aneurism, and while according to all physical indicators he seemed to be recovering well, on the inside he felt worse and worse. When he described this discomfort to his doctors, Hobson felt that his subjective experience of the aftermath of the stroke was completely ignored and that his doctors looked only at the data that indicated he was in good health. The pain that he suffered at this time led Hobson to apologize to his own patients. In the past, when their charts suggested they were fine or responding well to treatment, he had often disregarded the suffering they reported.

When Hobson suffered his second stroke, he began to wonder whether his father's genes were now speaking to him as they had once, he guessed, spoken to his father. Through his sense that the inherited genes were causing his illness, Hobson felt connected to his father in a new way. The progress of Hobson's clinical recovery after this second stroke very much resembled a psychological—or psychotherapeutic—process of working out his relationship with his father.

Anxiety over death in some cases can take the form of a question about the genes that were passed from the parent to the child, while in other cases anxiety involves fixating on the particular age at which a parent died. For example, a Russian man started experiencing strange attacks of breathlessness and at one point even fainted on the street.[10] When doctors could find no physical cause for his symptoms, he was sent to a psychiatric hospital. A consulting psychologist there asked about the man's family background and learned that his father had committed suicide at the age of thirty-nine. When the psychologist looked up the patient's age, she noticed that he was thirty-eight. In discussions with the patient, it became clear that the anxiety over dying at the same time as the father played an important role in this patient's inability to breathe.

Calvin Colarusso describes a similar case, that of Mr. B, who sought help through psychoanalysis because of acute anxiety over death.[11] This anxiety became especially pronounced when Mr. B turned forty-nine, since his father had died ten days before his fiftieth birthday. With this loss, the family suddenly fell into poverty. As an adult, Mr. B strove to build a successful and prosperous career in order to "bullet-proof his family" so that in case he died, they would not suffer the poverty that he did after his father's sudden death.

When Mr. B turned forty-nine, his physician noticed a significant lowering of his testosterone, which was taken as a possible cause of his depression. Mr. B was prescribed antidepressants, but these did not seem to help. On the fearful day when Mr. B turned fifty, his mother suddenly fell into a coma and died two days later. After this painful event, Mr. B started remembering how as a child he wished his father would die and how horrified he was when his wishes apparently came true with his father's premature death. But at one point in analysis he said, "I am beginning to see him as a man, not just my Dad." From then on, Mr. B slowly gave up on antidepressants and started feeling better. To his doctor's surprise, his testosterone levels also went back to normal.

The year before his fiftieth birthday, Mr. B, in a manner of speaking, started to "close everything down," and the falling levels of his testosterone were a physical sign of his "preparation" for death. The psychoanalyst took the change in testosterone as an unusual form of self-imposed "hormonal castration" related to Mr. B's infantile wishes to kill his father and take his place. One, however, also has to question what role his mother's death played in the lifting of Mr. B's anxiety. Did she in some way die instead of Mr. B? Did her death alter something with regard to the incestuous wishes he had fostered as a child?

If Hobson heard his father's genes as a voice that announced his own mortality, for Mr. B, it was the number fifty that was the herald of death. In both cases, the fear of death became fixated on an object of anxiety: in one case on the idea of genes taking control of life, and in the other case the prospect of reaching a certain age. The point to be taken here is that Hobson's anxieties about his genetic inheritance are no more or less "scientific" than Mr. B's profound concerns about his fiftieth birthday. Both men looked to the object of their anxiety as an explanatory cause of the state in which they found themselves.

Psychoanalysis and Genetics

People often consult a geneticist not because of a current illness but because they fear they are at risk of getting ill in the future. Psychoanalyst Andrée Lehman observed that women who consulted geneticists about their risk of getting breast cancer often already had concerns about their future or about the origin and transmissibility of genes. They were often full of doubt and un-certainty, hence already in the grip of anxiety. When these women were informed that they were in no danger of develop-ing genetically linked breast cancer, some seemed satisfied, evinced feelings of relief, proffered their thanks, and resolved to follow preventative recommendations. But others seemed just as anxious as before, if not more so. They would demand more tests or start focusing on other organs they feared might be-come cancerous in the future.[12]

Deciding to be tested for a genetic predisposition can be a troubling family affair. For example, in the film *Still Alice*, a middle-aged woman, Alice (played by Julianne Moore), is an ambitious professor of linguistics who suddenly starts losing her memory. Her neurologist diagnoses her with early-onset Alzheimer's disease with genetic roots. When Alice tells her grown-up children about her illness, she also informs them about the danger that they might have inherited the gene. The children are encouraged to get themselves tested; however, they are also warned that they may not want to know whether they have inherited a predisposition for their mother's illness. The oldest daughter, who is starting a family, decides to get tested since she wants to know whether she will pass it on to her future children. She also has high hopes that if the test is positive, medicine science will soon provide an early intervention to halt the progress of illness. The results of her test are positive but everything seems to be all right with the twins that she later delivers. Her brother tests negative, and the youngest daughter, Lydia, an aspiring actress, who in the end takes care of her ailing mother, decides against the test. The film does not explain the reasons for Lydia's willful ignorance in regard to her genes, but it does show that of all the family members, she shows the most attention to and compassion for their mother.

Some people find it hard to deal with genetic information. Even if they understand it, they may not be able to accept it. Where knowledge brings intellectual comprehension, it may still fail to override preexisting anxieties or beliefs. Psychoanalysts working with people with anxieties about cancer observe that cancer can evoke fantasies of both physical and mental decline, as well as abandonment and loss. These fantasies can be linked to how cancer is perceived within the larger family group. For some people, family relationships can be thoroughly revisited and thrown into turmoil when they go through genetic testing. They may suddenly remember certain past family events or particular sets of family beliefs, while others may engage with previously abandoned family traditions. While the younger generation may feel angry about the genes they have inherited, the older generation may feel guilty about passing on something bad to their offspring.

Although some people develop strategies that allow them to outright ignore important genetic information, others attempt to make the necessary cognitive adjustment by absorbing the knowledge but not seeing it as something that is fixed, certain, or determining. Problems arise when knowledge about genes is perceived as certain and when people strongly identify with the language of statistical likelihood in which genetic information is often presented.

The way doctors present unsettling information influences a patient's anxieties, but how the patient hears this information, or whether the patient listens at all, also makes a difference to his or her reaction.[13] The question, however, remains whether patients have the right to ignorance. Can they inform doctors in advance that they do not want to know when the news about their health is bad? Discussions about the right not to know are also part of ethical studies in the domain of genetics. While in

some cases people might willfully decide not to subject themselves to genetic testing or not to learn about its results, in other
cases, it might be that some knowledge about one's genes becomes available inadvertently through so-called incidental findings.[14] For example, when people agree to be part of scientific
research, they cannot easily opt out of learning about some
unexpected findings that come up in the research. The ethical
question is whether a person can inform the researcher in advance that he or she does not want to learn about incidental
findings. Is the doctor obliged to keep this promise in a case
where treatment may be possible for the disease that was discovered by accident? Geneticists also deal with dilemmas about
whether to transmit knowledge when they by chance discover
that family members are not genetically related. What if, when
a family volunteers to be part of some particular genetic research, the geneticist discovers that the parents are not genetically related to their child, and it is revealed that there had been
a mix-up in the hospital when the child was born? In any further
testing, the geneticist might decide not to tell the family about
such a discovery if no genetically transmitted illness is discovered among these volunteers. However, if the geneticist were to
discover one, he or she would be under pressure to inform the
family about this finding and also about the finding that they
are not genetically related.

Genes and Crime

As we have seen, for some people information about their
genes is linked to doubt and anxiety, but for others it presents
certainty—an answer, for example, not only to why they have
fallen ill with a certain disease but also to why they have behaved in a particular way. In the legal domain, genetics has

played an important role in the last decade in discussions about determinism and free will, as well as responsibility and punishment.

Some judicial cases nowadays call on expert witnesses in genetics who are brought in to testify that someone may have a genetic predisposition to commit criminal acts. One such example is the trial of Abdelmalek Bayout, an Algerian national, in Trieste, Italy, in 2009.[15] Bayout was accused of killing Walter Felipe Novoa Perez, who mocked the eye makeup Bayout was wearing for religious reasons. Bayout had been diagnosed with a mental disorder, and this diagnosis was taken into account as a mitigating factor when he was sentenced to nine years and two months in prison. Bayout appealed, and at his retrial an expert in genetics testified that the defendant may have been genetically predetermined to committing a violent crime. The expert pointed to changes in the *MAOA* gene, which regulates neurotransmitters, among them serotonin and dopamine. In reference to the studies that linked the malfunction of this gene to the tendency to be violent, the expert concluded that genes may have played a role in Bayout's behavior.[16] The court accepted this claim and further reduced the defendant's sentence.

In the last few decades, studies suggesting that there is a genetic predisposition to criminal behavior have been highly contested. Old debates about the relationship between nature and nurture have resurfaced in relation to epigenetics, and focus has shifted from the analysis of genes to the analysis of how the environment affects the expression of genes.

In the United States, the idea that there might be a genetic determination toward violence gained strength after the publication of forensic psychologist Adrian Raine's book *The Anatomy of Violence*.[17] As an example of the genetic predisposition for violence, Raine takes the case of Jeffrey Landrigan, a man who was put on death row for two different murders and whose biological father had received the same sentence for similar crimes.

Landrigan's case presents a disturbing history of violence and criminality in a single family. Landrigan's great-grandfather was a bootlegger. His son, Landrigan's grandfather, died in a shootout with the police while he was robbing a bank; and his own son, Darrel Hill, observed this shootout. Later, Hill also became a criminal. He committed two murders and was sentenced to death. Hill had a son called Billy whom he saw only when he was a baby. When Billy was six months old, his mother abandoned him in a day care center.[18] Billy was later adopted into a family, where some reports claim that he was well taken care of and loved, while others point out that his adoptive mother was an alcoholic and often aggressive toward the child. This adoptive family changed Billy's name to Jeffrey. From his youth on, Landrigan had problems with drugs and alcohol; and he ended up being placed in various institutions for delinquent youngsters. As an adult, Landrigan killed two people, as his biological father, Darrel Hill, had, and was also sentenced to death.

Hill, on death row, said about his biological son, "I don't think there can be any doubt in anyone's mind that he (Jeffrey Landrigan) was fulfilling his destiny. . . . I believe that when he was conceived, what I was, he became. . . . The last time I saw him he was a baby in a bed, and underneath his mattress I had two .38 pistols and Demerol; that's what he was sleeping on."[19]

Raine concludes, "Placing that gun and drugs under his baby boy's pillow foreshadowed what was to come. Like father, like son—whether it is violence, drugs, or alcohol. Landrigan was seemingly doing little more in life than acting out the sins of his biological father."[20] For Raine the fact that Landrigan was later adopted and, according to Raine's accounts, loved could not change the biological determinism of his genetic makeup.

Landrigan's story can, however, be interpreted in other ways. First, there is the possibility of brain damage resulting from his mother's substance abuse throughout her pregnancy. This was discussed in 2007 at the US Supreme Court's ruling over Landrigan's case, which examined whether Landrigan had been effectively represented by his court-appointed counsel when he was sentenced to death in his 1990 trial because Landrigan did not allow mitigating circumstances to be used in his defense and had also refused to let his ex-wife and mother testify on his behalf.[21] When the case ended at the Supreme Court, the majority of justices upheld Landrigan's convictions but four justices dissented, and in their argument the question of biological as well as psychological components of Landrigan's crime featured prominently. Justice John Paul Stevens, writing for the four dissenters in the Supreme Court, laid heavy blame on Landrigan's counsel for not ordering a psychological evaluation of Landrigan, which "would have uncovered a serious organic brain disorder." Stevens criticized the counsel for not consulting an expert to explore the effects of the drinking and drug use of the respondent's birth mother during pregnancy. In addition, Stevens called attention to the counsel's failure to present the history of Landrigan's troubled childhood with his adoptive family, which resulted in his youth being "marked by physical and emotional abuse, neglect by his adoptive parents, his own substance abuse problems[,] . . . a stunted education, and recurrent placement in substance abuse rehabilitation facilities, a psychiatric ward, and police custody."[22] This summary also emphasizes the interaction between genes and environmental factors.

A psychoanalytic approach, however, would focus on Landrigan's psychological identification with his father and not their genetic link. From various accounts it is known that Landrigan spent years trying to track down his biological father, Darrel Hill, and found him not long after Landrigan committed his first murder. Landrigan, who was twenty years old, had just come out of prison and married, and he would soon learn that he was going to become a father. One day, he went drinking with a childhood friend, Greg Brown, whom he had earlier asked to be godfather to his unborn child. A verbal fight ensued between the two when Brown called Landrigan a "punk," and Landrigan stabbed his friend to death.

Landrigan was sentenced to life in prison, but on appeal his sentence was reduced to twenty years.[23] When he was serving his sentence, a fellow prisoner told him that in his previous prison he had met a person who looked similar to Landrigan. When Landrigan established contact with this man, he learned that he was his biological father, Hill. Thus Landrigan had found his father by going to prison for committing a crime, and the two men started exchanging letters when they were serving sentences in different prisons.

Landrigan may have felt that people expected him to follow in his father's footsteps, since in his adopted family and in his school it was well known that he was the son of a criminal. One should also not neglect the fact that as a little baby, Landrigan was already caught in the web of anxiety related to breaking the law. The fact that his father was hiding two .38-caliber pistols and Demerol under the baby's mattress could have had important consequences for the child's development. Children can be influenced by their caregivers in many different direct ways; and in unconscious ways, they can also notice and take on the anxieties present in their caregivers. Even a two-year-old may be aware that adults who put guns under his mattress do not feel safe, and their insecurity can become his own fear. We should pay equal attention, moreover, to the fundamental lack of care for the child that the guns in this story represent. Psychopathic character traits have been traced to brain injuries suffered in childhood *and* to chronic neglect on the part of caregivers who fail to interact with and demonstrate concern for the infant at the symbiotic stage of development.

The term "father" plays an essential role in Landrigan's story. He committed his first killing when he was about to become a father, and he killed the man who was to become his child's godfather. These facts may have important ramifications for a psychoanalytic understanding of this crime. While Landrigan spent much of his youth searching for his biological father, the moment when he himself was about to become a father may have triggered something in him that contributed to his violent outburst toward the man who was supposed to take on the symbolic paternal role of a godfather.

Hill had also long been haunted by his own father, whom Hill had seen shot dead by police, and the man would often appear to Hill in hallucinations. Already in his youth, he was hearing the voice of his father telling him that he could not escape being killed, which is why he should kill first. Another preoccupation for both father and son may have been homosexual impulses. Hill, like Landrigan, became enraged when someone called him a "punk" in prison. After the insult, Hill stabbed this man to death, later claiming that he acted in self-defense against a sexual approach.

When Landrigan was serving his sentence, despite his murder charge he was put in a minimum-security work crew, which allowed him to escape from the prison facility. Once outside, his first desire was to find his biological mother, who lived in

Yuma, Arizona. On his way to Yuma, Landrigan stopped off in Phoenix, where he met a man named Chester Dyer who worked in a health club and was known for picking up men and having sex with them at his home. A few days later, Dyer was found strangled by an electrical cord and stabbed to death in his apartment. A deck of pornographic cards depicting naked men in sexual poses was strewn over the bed, with the ace of hearts propped up on Dyer's back. Police rearrested Landrigan when he was caught robbing a petrol station. His shoe prints matched those found at the scene of Dyer's murder. Landrigan denied killing Dyer; he claimed that Dyer had made sexual advances toward him but that another man had murdered him.

In their account of the Landrigan story, Dan Malone and Howard Swindle ask, "Do chromosomal cards dealt at birth determine whether a person becomes a sociopath or a productive member of society? Or does the world in which the child is reared cast the mould that forms the adult?"[24] Some theorists understand Landrigan as a genetically predetermined criminal; others see his acts as being similarly predetermined by social background. Neither explanation accounts for the very particular form of enjoyment he may have experienced while committing his crime. His murder of Dyer was highly idiosyncratic, artful even, rather than a raw response to present conditions in biology or culture. His neat and highly demonstrative arrangement of the playing cards at Dyer's home suggests that Landrigan was not simply a tool in the hands of some higher power—his genes, for example—but that he was very much a subject who wanted to leave a symbolic mark at the scene of his crime.

Rather than following the dictations of a line of genetic code, Landrigan might have committed this act as an attempt to confront such determinants. He was working within the family tradition of violence but modified the unthinking brutality of his father and grandfather with a viciously sophisticated strain of criminal behavior that was quite his own.

A geneticist's—or even a sociologist's—view of the Landrigan family's criminality fails to recognize such distinctions between the actions of one generation and those of another. Criminal acts, from the genetic point of view, are simply "criminal," to a lesser or greater extent. A police psychologist, or even a detective with a broader view of things, knows otherwise. Different criminal acts—different murders—often play out very different psychological dramas and preoccupations. Unlike his criminal forebears, Landrigan at some level understood that his life was largely about a search for something or someone with which or with whom he could identify. He was executed in 2010, and his final words were, "Boomer Sooner," the rallying cry for the supporters of the University of Oklahoma football team, the Sooners.

Genes: Information about What?

Molecular biology borrowed the term "program" from computer science to describe the genetic information an organism may contain. The term "information" tells us that we are dealing with something that is semantic data that can be communicated. We can also easily get the impression that this information works as an imperative or as a cause: if we possess information, we can interpret or suppress it, act on it or ignore it. In addition, advances in science raise hope that we will soon be able to control or amend our genes. One of the founders of the Human Genome Project, for example, said that with the decoding of the genome, for the first time a living creature can understand its origins and can undertake to design its future. Evelyn

Fox Keller also concluded that when life is relocated in the genes and redefined in terms of their informational content, the project of refashioning life, or redirecting the future course of evolution, can be cast as a manageable, doable project.[25]

We live in times of the so-called neurogenetic real. While we may hope to find truth in the body, we forget that human subjectivity—with its imagination, fantasies, self-damaging behavior, and *jouissance* related to transgression—cannot be reduced to a genetic code or a neuronal machine driven by the complex firing patterns of the cells in our brains. New knowledge related to the body is, however, affecting the way people relate to their bodies and to their ancestors. In addition to the new fantasies that people form around genes, the sense of identification is undergoing a change. In the cases of "wrongful birth," the children and their parents may take the genes related to the wrong donor as the determining factor of children's behavior and may attribute any mental problems or unruliness to the donor's genes. However, it is also possible that—all genes aside—a particular child may start identifying with or otherwise follow in the footsteps of the biological father whether he was an anonymous sperm donor or a father who later abandoned the child.

When genetic science stresses the importance of epigenetics by acknowledging that the ultimate impact of the effect of the genes depends on social and environmental factors, it also emphasizes the power of the family and other intersubjective relationships in a person's life. Even studies that try to establish a genetic basis for the kind of impulsive behavior that breaks the law point out that an unstable emotional environment at home, and especially domestic abuse, triggers the activity of the genes linked to impulsivity. Such studies, however, need to take into account how a proliferation of media stories often reduce complex genetic research findings to exaggerated claims that we have found the "gene for criminal behavior." Such claims have a significant effect on the subject's body, unconscious fantasies, and identifications. With the spread of the belief that genes are responsible for crime, we are creating an epigenetic setting—language and culture—that any study of genes and behavior needs to take into account.

4

Denial of Illness

WHEN MARIA HAD TERRIBLE stomach pains, her first thought was food poisoning. She blamed the restaurant where she had eaten lunch and regretted finishing the meal, which had tasted odd. After a few hours the pain became excruciating, and Maria ended up in the emergency room, where an ultrasound revealed a huge mass in her abdomen. She underwent surgery to remove a large tumor from her colon. When Maria woke up, she was told that she had suffered from an ileus and that a pathologist's report would determine whether it was malignant.

Maria was relieved to hear the word "ileus." Not long before, a friend had been diagnosed with an ileus and made a speedy recovery. At the time, Maria had understood an ileus as being not cancer but rather a benign mass that blocks the colon. She seized on the diagnosis and completely ignored the doctor's warning about pathology findings. For Maria, the term "ileus" became an explanation for all kinds of previous troubles—occasional indigestion, a feeling of fullness, and lack of appetite. In addition, she often told her friends and family how lucky she was that she had only developed an ileus, while many other patients on her hospital ward were stricken with cancer.

When the doctor gave Maria the results of the biopsy, she did not allow him to explain anything. As soon as he uttered the word "adenocarcinoma," Maria interrupted him with her spiel about the ileus, boasting of her luck in not having cancer and expressing sympathy for those who had to deal with a cancer diagnosis. Her frantic monologue prevented the doctor from having the chance to explain to Maria that her ileus actually was a form of colon cancer, which luckily had not spread to the adjacent organs. This was why, for the time being, no further therapy was suggested. When Maria was discharged, she was given a document explaining this information in detail. She never read it.

Maria's husband was well aware of his wife's diagnosis. He was shocked to observe that his wife, who was exceptionally bright and eager to learn new things, found such solace in denial. Uncertain as to whether he should compel her to acknowledge her real condition or allow her to maintain her self-deception, he discussed his concerns with an online community of people whose partners were cancer patients. One day he asked how to get someone who is in denial about their illness to confront the truth. An anonymous doctor responded by drawing an analogy to eating. People taste new, unknown types of food in many ways: some courageously swallow a mouthful, while others look the unknown morsel over and take a nibble with great caution. Sometimes they try another bite, and sometimes they turn away in horror, never wanting to come near it again. It is much the same with people facing a life-threatening illness, the doctor said. Some want to know all about it; they dig into their illness with gusto, research it, and talk about it. Others, though, proceed with caution; they may try learning just a little and then stop. Still others find any level of information or exploration too distressing and thus create all kinds of protective mechanisms to shield themselves from learning anything scary or unpleasant.

Maria fell into the last group of people. She continued talking about her ileus, and soon people around her stopped asking about her illness. Even her doctors never mentioned that her ileus was a form of cancer. To protect herself from any possible future cancer diagnosis, she religiously took various vitamins and became a passionate believer in the powers of certain herbs she bought in an Asian pharmacy—all with the idea of preventing herself from getting cancer in the future. She never suffered from a recurrence of her symptoms.

It is possible to speculate that in some way Maria "knew" she had cancer but found various strategies to protect herself from this unbearable knowledge. The word "ileus" was for Maria a magical word—what anthropologists describe as a word with a special power to protect a person from danger.

Maria protected herself from the truth of her illness, first by refusing to listen to the doctor's explanation and then by not reading the doctor's report. Another part of her defense strategy was to pass all her anxiety onto her husband. When she enclosed herself in a bubble of willful ignorance, her husband assumed the burden of the knowledge she did not want to acknowledge. And by allowing Maria to remain ignorant of the truth, he helped alleviate her anxiety. In addition, he further shielded Maria by encouraging other people to avoid the subject of cancer when she was present.

This case suggests that the ability of an individual to maintain his or her ignorance, willful or otherwise, is dependent on others being willing to collude in protecting that ignorance. This is the same strategy that can be seen at work in many cases of ignorance and denial. When others play along with a person's choice of denial as a tactic for avoiding unsettling information, that person's anxiety is transferred onto others. In the case of another couple who were also dealing with the threat of cancer, the anxiety was diffused by the wife doing all the talking about her husband's illness. They were both highly educated people, but after his diagnosis the husband took on the role of a child. The wife was always the one who explained to other people the medical procedures that he had undergone, and she boasted about her cooking skills, which she claimed had helped build up his strength. She also repeatedly and compulsively told friends how happy she was that her husband did not suffer from cancer. In the presence of the doctors who knew that the opposite was true, the wife would discourse in great detail on the benign nature of her husband's illness and never gave any hint that she might know the truth. In order to maintain this illusion she relied on having knowledgeable interlocutors whose muteness and seeming acceptance of her monologues supported her explanation. The husband was often silent during these speeches, nodding approvingly as his wife described his condition. It was unclear whether he was also in denial or whether he was just trying to protect his wife from the anxiety the truth would cause her. Happily, he did not require aggressive treatment, so his wife was able to continue to avoid acknowledging the serious nature of her husband's health problems.

In the domain of medicine, strategies of denial and ignorance have changed somewhat in recent decades, as "informed consent" procedures have been implemented and medical staff have faced increasing pressure to inform patients about the nature of their conditions and the potential risks of treatment, as I shall discuss later.

A change in the way people deny life-threatening illness has also occurred as a result of general changes in the way that human agency is perceived in postindustrial, capitalist society.

Widespread ideas of choice and the belief in the power of rational decision-making have contributed to this change and the idea that individuals need to take responsibility for their illness and its treatment.[1] In the case of cancer this is sometimes expressed as the idea that people get cancer because they have not followed a healthy lifestyle or because they have had a negative outlook on life that has somehow resulted in cancer. It is perhaps not surprising that sometimes people seek to avoid such judgments by denying there is anything wrong with them. Since there is an important link between denial and people's anxieties about death, new technologies have also stimulated new ways of denying death—indeed, in some quarters they have fostered fantasies of immortality, as we shall see later in this chapter, which are differently played out by transhumanists who hope to extend human life by merging human bodies with machines, biohackers who are working on intervening in the body so that it can live longer, and various immortalist movements that claim that people can overcome death by the power of their belief in the possibility of endless life and especially by interacting with others who embrace the idea of immortality.[2]

The Power of Denial

While ignorance and denial are overwhelmingly significant factors in matters of health, medical science has paid attention to them only sporadically. People might ignore certain medical knowledge, such as scientific research on vaccination; however, when it comes to problems with their own health, they are more prone to denial, a psychological defense mechanism that kicks in when they are unable to deal with something that is traumatic.

The most substantive work on the problem of denial in medicine was carried out in the 1980s by Shlomo Breznitz, who tackled the question of denial in heart attack patients.[3] Breznitz encountered seven different kinds of denial among his patients, many of whom went from one type of denial to another as their illnesses progressed, often regressing to a more "primitive form of denial."[4]

The first type of denial mentioned in Breznitz's study involves a negation of personal relevance. An example here is a group of coronary patients who witnessed a fellow patient suffer a fatal cardiac arrest in the hospital. The majority of these observers did not think that something similar could also happen to them even though they were at high risk. The second type of denial Breznitz identified is a denial of urgency. This happens when people who have experienced previous health emergencies (such as a heart attack or cancer) delay calling for help when their symptoms recur.[5] Breznitz's third type involves the denial of vulnerability by people who feel protected from another crisis because they have changed their lifestyle (exercising more, eating more healthily, and so on); others may give up all sense of responsibility and perceive a heart attack as simply a matter of luck, fate, destiny, or some other uncontrollable factor. Other forms of denial included blocking out factual and practical information, sometimes to the extent that patients indiscriminately denied all information about their illness by escaping into their own world, creating delusions about their health that enabled them to hold themselves together.

In addition to the types of denial Breznitz identified, changes in the way society perceives the meaning and purpose of work, and people's altered sense of agency about their jobs and their lives in general, have given rise to new types of denial about health. The ideology of late capitalism puts people under pressure to be continuously productive and entrepreneurial, as well as self-critical about any lack of success. Glorification of work as an idea and a practice goes far beyond mere employment and is expressed in the elevation of self-improvement as an ideal. One is supposed to endlessly work on oneself and on one's relationships, friendships, parenting skills, and so on. It is important to keep working and not fall ill, and if illness strikes, it is urgent to work on getting better. Not working can harm a person's sense of identity and worth; doctors often hear patients say, "I am nothing without my work." Cardiologists have observed that heart attack patients are less likely to ask how long they will need to rest than how long it will be before they can return to work.[6] The desire to return to work from sick leave as soon as possible has led to a new form of denial of illness. People who are unwell may intellectually understand the nature of their illness while also being in denial that it may impinge on their ability to continue working long and arduous hours.

A related form of denial that results from our work-obsessed ideology is linked to the perception of recovery from illness as a particular kind of work that must be engaged in with extreme determination. On being discharged after a heart attack, some patients will immediately try to change their lives with new personal regimens. They will begin exercising too strenuously too soon, throw themselves into extreme sports, or become obsessed with monitoring their diets to the point of developing orthorexia. Intensive work on recovery becomes a way of ignoring the impact that an illness has already had on the body and can cause physical stress that is actually counterproductive if not positively dangerous for people with heart ailments and other disorders.

Psychoanalysts have also reported on something that can be called "split-day" denial.[7] During the day, a patient will take scrupulous care of his or her health—count calories, eat nothing but organic food, exercise consistently and rigorously—but in the evening that person will flip into a completely different mode, drinking to excess, taking drugs, and displaying a total disregard for "normal," healthy behavior. "Split-day" individuals may even deny that drugs are harmful, or claim that alcohol and cigarettes will have no serious impact on their health, thanks to the strict regimens they follow during the day.

Agnosognosia and the Inability to Fall Ill

The most striking cases of patients "splitting off" from, or ignoring, their illness involve a neurological disorder known as "agnosognosia" (also spelled anosognosia).[8] Those who present with this disorder are unable to acknowledge a particular neurological deficit. For example, one person may refuse to admit that a part of his or her body is paralyzed, while another may not notice that he or she is wearing only one shoe or is only partly dressed. People with agnosognosia may be oblivious to the unusual way in which they put food in their mouths, or to the fact that they chew only on one side or eat from just one half of the plate. A man may shave only one half of his face, read half the words in front of him, or draw just half of an image. Some people even experience a particular kind of alienation from parts of their body—feeling, for example, that their legs do not belong to them. The most interesting cases of agnosognosia concern denial of blindness. Some people with brain lesions that affect their eyesight deny their loss of vision and act as if they are actually able to see. Visual agnosognostics who have problems orienting themselves in space and dealing with daily tasks often not only fail to report that they do not see but also will blame their difficulties on their surroundings, saying, for example, that the light is not strong enough or there is something wrong with their glasses.

While some agnosognostics are in complete denial of their illness, others show mere indifference, and still others accuse doctors of exaggeration or error. In the 1960s, Edwin Weinstein and Malvin Cole explained agnosognosia as something that involves more than a physiological or neurological condition.[9] They looked at the denial of illness or disability in the context of broader defense mechanisms, as unconscious strategies that help people push aside what they cannot psychologically accept. Weinstein and Cole observed that some patients suffering from agnosognosia devised alternative explanations for why they ended up in the hospital. Some said that they were there just to visit friends, while others claimed that they worked there. People who had been paralyzed by an accident or a stroke sometimes invented alternative explanations: their limbs were simply lazy or tired; or they were unable to move because they were sore after injections.

Weinstein and Cole also observed that some patients denied not only their paralysis but also incontinence, vomiting, and a whole range of seemingly undeniable bodily symptoms. Surprisingly, while denying their illness, for the most part they placidly accepted hospital ward routines, medications, and even surgery. Weinstein and Cole advanced the interesting hypothesis that patients will select and "screen" what symptoms they recognize in order to redefine their situation and strike a balance between the reality of their new needs and challenges, and their former social roles.[10]

The observations of Weinstein and Cole add an important dimension to neurological research on agnosognosia because they take into account the highly subjective ways people deal with neurological impairment. More recently, Catherine Morin looked at the way stroke victims create highly individual fantasies around their paralysis.[11] Two people suffering similar brain damage will tell themselves and others very different stories about their symptoms. In these stories, an individual's unconscious plays an important part: long-forgotten memories and traumas from childhood are interwoven into the new self-perceptions produced by neurological impairment. One patient who suffered from agnosognosia and had a paralyzed arm believed that his limp arm belonged to his dead brother. A memory related to the terrible loss of his brother seems to have become intertwined with the patient's experience of physical loss. Another person with a similarly handicapped arm, though, said that it felt like a hug that he remembered receiving as a young boy from his father. In both cases, the incapacitated limb became linked to old memories and long-forgotten emotions.

Another condition in which people deny or ignore what is happening to their bodies is described by psychiatrist Herman Musaph as "pathological health." The idea that something might be wrong with their mind or their body presents a form of "narcissistic injury" to such people, so they will deny or downplay any physical symptoms and never complain if they are feeling less than perfect. This kind of denial is sometimes called counterhypochondria, as it is the mirror image of the condition of hypochondriacs, who go to great lengths to exaggerate their symptoms and are always claiming that they are ill.[12]

Informed Consent

In classical Greek philosophy, truth was thought of as "like a medicine," to be prescribed to the "patient" in carefully controlled amounts, and until recently it was standard medical practice to take a similar approach to the truth.[13] Doctors believed that too much truth was potentially unsettling for the patient, and so their communications were characterized by evasion, nondisclosure, and concealment. Carefully maintained ignorance on the part of patients and discretion on the part of doctors was generally seen as being integral to the effective practice of medicine, as well as maintaining professional authority and mystique. Such secrecy and lack of transparency was also useful whenever it was necessary to cover up a doctor's uncertainty, mistakes, or ignorance. If doctors did tell the truth about someone's condition, they told it to their relatives, the "next of kin," and then strongly advised them not to tell the patient.

These attitudes changed in the 1970s.[14] With new approaches to medical ethics and the proliferation of legal cases in the domain of medicine, informed consent became an important part of medical practice.[15] The underlying assumption of informed consent is that people are "rational subjects" who can assess information impartially and then make an informed decision about their well-being. This relies on the expectation that a person who consents to a particular course of action has clearly understood all of its potential consequences.

The idea of informed consent emerged as a result of various abuses in the field of medicine. The most notorious, historically, were the medical experiments performed in Nazi Germany on prisoners in concentration camps. Cases have come to light more recently across the globe of people (most often prisoners, minorities, the poor, the disenfranchised, and the powerless) being deceived or coerced into taking part in medical research or into selling their organs for cash and not being properly informed about the possible or probable consequences of procedures to which they would be subjected. Such abuses contributed to the demand that consent be made central to the patient-professional relationship, in treatment as well as research. The idea of informed consent was also championed by those who sought to challenge the paternalism that is traditionally inherent in the patient-doctor relationship, and by campaigns for greater patient autonomy.[16]

While medical ethicists have addressed many of the issues related to informed consent, including what legally and practically constitutes informed consent, they rarely touch on the conscious and unconscious mechanisms that guide people in their decision-making or the fact that sometimes people simply refuse to accept responsibility for making such decisions.[17] Debates on informed consent can also neglect the fact that a patient may embrace ignorance, and the authority issuing the consent form may collude with them in doing so.

In most jurisdictions, for a statement of informed consent to be legally valid, the person signing it needs to be understood to be "of right mind," to use a somewhat outdated expression. In other words, the person has to be capable of making a rational decision that contributes to his or her well-being. More than a century of psychological and psychoanalytical research, however, has shown that "rationality" is a highly subjective and thus contentious principle.[18] Even if one were able to agree that rational courses of action should, generally speaking, seek to maximize pleasure (or comfort and well-being) and minimize pain (or discomfort and ill health), thousands of psychoanalytic cases demonstrate that people often fail to behave according to this definition of rationality—especially when facing troubling choices or periods of stress. Instead the individual's unconscious will seize on tactics—inspired sometimes by infantile convictions, magical thinking, or deeply fixed, personal aversions—that defy legal or scientific protocols and so-called rational choices. Standards for informed consent are therefore based on ideals about human rationality and pragmatism that observation does not bear out.

Accepting a standard definition of rationality is a necessary prerequisite for modern-day contracts (including informed consent) between patient and doctor (or patient and medical institution). As a result, in highly litigious enterprises, informed consent has inspired new forms of ignorance on the part of the patient. When patients agree to a medical procedure, they are asked to sign a document stating that they understand and accept all kinds of terrible possible outcomes. Most people will usually take a quick glance through the text and sign the form without fully, "rationally" digesting it, which raises questions about the nature of the information the consent form contains. To the lay observer, informed consent forms are worded so as to protect the provider of the service in case something goes wrong with the procedure. That protection is arguably justified, since no procedure and no individual physician will ever be infallible. But at the same time it can lead to a patient having an unrealistic confidence in the power and skill of those treating him or her because the consent form rarely, if ever, gives information about the professional who will be treating the patient. Justin Oakley proposes that people who are deciding whether to go ahead with an operation should have access to information about complications and bad outcomes from previous surgeries conducted by their surgeon.[19] Even in countries where the national health system does not allow individuals a choice of doctor, access to records of surgeon-specific performance would allow patients to give (or withhold) consent in a more informed way. To support his claims, Oakley cites examples of Australian doctors whose records of incompetent service should have disqualified them from further practice but who somehow were allowed to continue. Even when colleagues knew or suspected a particular surgeon's long-standing malpractice, they kept quiet about it in a professional conspiracy of silence that is repeated far too often. Although, one might well argue that a patient has a right to be informed about a doctor's or a hospital's track record long before treatment is imminent.

Can the Truth Hurt?

While many of the problems in doctor-patient relationships arise from the way the truth is sometimes concealed, distorted, or avoided, telling patients the truth can have very positive effects.[20] One study followed the reactions of people told just before treatment that the trainee nurse or junior doctor performing the procedure would be doing so for the first time.[21] The study was carried out in an emergency department where medical students were performing tasks such as suturing wounds and inserting intravenous lines. Most patients wanted to know whether the student had done these tasks before, but when informed that he or she had not, the majority still agreed to let the student go ahead anyway. Many of those who gave their consent were not threatened by the student's lack of experience and appreciated his or her honesty. A friend of mine who was injured by a grenade in the Bosnian war had a similar response. He ended up in a temporary clinic with a severely injured arm, where a young surgeon told him that his arm might be saved if tissue were transplanted from his leg. The surgeon admitted, however, that he had never performed the operation. He also pointed out that if it failed, my friend could suffer more than if he just had his arm amputated. This admission of limited knowledge and ability by the doctor actually persuaded my friend to go ahead with the riskier operation. The transplant worked and his arm was saved. But even if the procedure hadn't worked, my friend would probably not have blamed the young doctor for trying, since he felt he had been given all the facts and therefore been adequately informed of the potential risks.

When it comes to their own health, doctors are just as likely to resort to denial as anyone else. In his book *When Breath Becomes Air*, the neurosurgeon Paul Kalanithi recounts his battle with terminal cancer and how he at first ignored his symptoms.[22] Toward the end of his residency he started losing weight, experiencing pains of all kinds, and feeling generally unwell. His desire to finally become a fully qualified neurosurgeon, however, was so strong that for months he ignored these symptoms and neglected his own health. Kalanithi persuaded himself that he was simply overworked and that he would get better once his training was complete, but tragically he died at the age of thirty-seven. A similar case, but one with a more positive outcome, involved a young Slovenian medical student who suffered from terrible headaches but again ignored his symptoms, thinking that they were just the result of exhaustion from long hours of study. Although he was studying to be a doctor, he pursued various alternative therapies and resisted seeking a medical explanation for his condition until he was finally persuaded to have an MRI scan, which revealed a large mass growing under his skull. He was diagnosed with a rare type of tumor that the neurosurgeon assigned to his case had never treated before, but when the student asked for another surgeon who did have the relevant experience, the surgeon refused to recognize his own lack of experience and tried to stop the student from being transferred to a different clinic. Luckily the student was successfully operated on by another neurosurgeon and finished his studies, though he decided not to practice medicine. In this case we have two types of denial: the medical student initially denied he needed medical treatment, and the neurosurgeon denied his lack of expertise.

Denial of Mortality

Freud believed that denial was linked to our fear of death. He argued that denial is an unconscious defense mechanism that helps people to deal with this fear, while the unconscious itself, in Freud's opinion, does not recognize the possibility of its own death—it acts as if it were immortal.[23] Jacques Lacan also thought that it is as impossible to think about our own death as it is to think about our own birth.[24] As a result, birth and death raise questions that we answer for the most part with the help of a fantasy, a story that can only provide temporary solace.

For some people, denial of their own mortality or denial of previous trauma may become so entrenched in the way they think about both life and death that they test the limits between life and death by engaging in dangerous, life-threatening activities such as extreme sports or developing a risky lifestyle. Perhaps one of the most common forms of such risk taking is engaging in unprotected sex, which took an extreme form in the "gift-giving parties" that were held in some gay circles in the United States during the height of the AIDS epidemic.[25] Uninfected men engaged in anonymous sex with strangers, many of whom were HIV positive. For some men, such exposure to infection was a way to deal with anxiety about HIV, a kind of Russian roulette. For those who felt that it was just a matter of time before they got sick, it was a deliberate surrender to the virus, since there was no point battling against it or trying to avoid it.[26] Many strongly identified with friends or partners who were already infected and did not want to stand out by not having HIV. For some, however, gift-giving parties were a ritual through which they played out their denial of death or tried to demonstrate their mastery of the fear of death.

Rarely a solitary pursuit, denial of death often involves other people, as well as a broader social setting. In his memoir about his mother, Susan Sontag, David Rieff writes that at the end of her life, she and her doctor shared a fantasy that they could halt her demise with new, aggressive treatments.[27] Sontag was known for liking to be in charge of her life, and her strong will usually allowed her to "get what she wanted." Rieff describes how, in making medical decisions in her last months, her persistence was coupled with and doubled by her doctor's belief in medical science. Although her body was very weak, she decided to undergo a bone marrow transplant. Her desire to live and her belief in the possibility of a cure meant that she ignored the inability of her body to endure such aggressive treatment. Rieff stresses that his mother was not in denial about her illness; rather she refused to accept death and "could not imagine giving in . . . to the imperative of dying."[28]

In the late 1960s, in her seminal work on dying, Elisabeth Kübler-Ross noted that there was a symbiotic relationship between the doctor's and the patient's need for denial. She observed that doctors who embraced denial also encouraged it in their patients, while those who could talk more easily with their patients about the terminal nature of their illness enabled their patients to speak more openly as well.[29] Avery Weisman, who spent decades analyzing illness and denial, observed how relationships with significant people affected when and with whom denial occurs.[30] People sometimes feel able to speak frankly about their illness with a complete stranger but are unable to do so with close family or friends. While they may appear to be in denial, they are actually fully aware of what is happening, but by not talking about their illness, they may be trying to avoid upsetting those they are close to or trying to preserve the relationships they had before they fell ill.

Denial as Choice?

While studies in the field of denial and medicine over the first half of the twentieth century often referenced psychoanalytic theories of denial, especially in connection to fear of death, more recent studies tend to perceive denial as a choice.[31] The evolving discourse on patients' rights has led to the argument that denial should be considered a matter of rational decision. In this view, denial is no longer perceived exclusively as something related to one's awareness of illness or the emotions related to illness and its potentially painful consequences; rather, it is primarily taken as a conscious choice to protect one's privacy. Denial becomes a matter of communication: a patient, for example, *decides* to talk about his or her illness with some people but not with others. A new point of view argues that when people face life-threatening illness and yet never mention it, this reticence should be taken not as denial linked to anxiety but rather as a conscious choice not to discuss death.[32]

While people have always embraced denial in one form or another as a way to deal with impending death, the new notion of denial as a choice makes denial appear "healthy" or at least rational for the first time. It becomes a tactic, often temporary, that allows patients to come to terms with death at their own pace and in their own way. It allows patients to preserve their own sense of identity rather than being defined by their imminent mortality.[33]

The way denial is treated in an institution such as a hospice very much relies on the broader social understandings of the time, so when a particular paradigm becomes established, it can bring with it new forms of social control.[34] In the 1980s, at the height of the popularity of Kübler-Ross's writing on dying, palliative care workers observed that patients were often expected to follow the five stages of grief described in the book. If they did not appear to be "transitioning" from anger to acceptance (for example), it was almost as if they were not progressing toward their death in the proper fashion. More recently we have seen emerging pressure on dying people to participate in the planning of their death, with those who do not want to being criticized for not "owning" the finale of their lives. People who are trying to subvert death denial are organizing death salons and death cafés where the public can openly discuss death, and some are hoping that a "death-positive conversation game" will allow friends and family to start the difficult conversation about death and dying.[35]

We not only have trouble accepting that death will "happen" to us, but also that it will claim the people we love. Hans Kristian Rausing was prosecuted in 2012 for hiding the body of his deceased wife, Eva, for two months under a pile of clothes in their bedroom.[36] Eva's hidden body was found accidentally when Hans was stopped by police for dangerous driving. The police discovered that he was intoxicated, and on top of the drugs in his car, they also found a pile of old letters addressed to Eva. A search of his mansion later revealed Eva's decomposed body, and he was charged under an old British statute that criminalized the failure to give the deceased proper and timely burial.

At the trial, it was revealed that the couple had both been drug addicts and when Eva died from heart failure as a result of taking drugs, Hans could not accept that she was gone; he could not "let her leave." From a psychoanalytical point of view, the use of the old British law was an apt response to Hans's denial. It was not that Hans was delusional and did not admit that Eva had died; rather, he did everything he could to literally not see the reality of her death. As the counsel for defense at his trial pointed out, Hans couldn't deal with reality and also could not face telling anyone else what had happened. Publicly announcing Eva's death would have been a symbolic act, and registering her death with the authorities would have been an act of acknowledging the reality that Hans could not face.

Choosing Immortality

While it is not uncommon for people to be in denial about their own deaths or those of their loved ones, technology now offers ever new ways to express it. While some still believe in having their bodies cryogenically frozen—or maybe just their heads or brains (ready for insertion into a new body constructed at some indefinite point in the future), others are using new technologies to keep the deceased symbolically "alive."[37] With the help of Adobe Photoshop one can, for example, "age" the picture of someone who died before old age or even before adulthood. People who have lost a child thus have a way of seeing what their child would have looked like had he or she lived to an older age. One can also use a computer program to create new speech from recordings of someone made before their death. The program creates the illusion that one is listening to the deceased person. As the maker of this program says, "Through a combination of audio-video recordings, speech recognition software, and machine learning, one can ask a question of a departed family member and receive a response, creating the illusion they're still alive and well."[38] More complex interaction with the dead is possible with the help of digital avatars that are made in the image of the deceased. In 2016, South Korean mother Jang Ji-sung lost her seven-year-old daughter Nayeon to an incurable disease. But three years later, this mother was able to interact with her daughter in the online world. With the help of artificial intelligence, the mother was able to talk to the avatar made in the image of her dead daughter. The mother found solace in the interaction. She said, "I met Nayeon, who called me with a smile, for a very short time, but it's a very happy time. I think I've had the dream I've always wanted."[39] One wonders whether these kinds of interactions will change the way people mourn the loss of their loved ones. People who find solace in interacting with the avatars of the dead do not deny that these people are dead. Nor are they ignoring what has happened to them. Rather, they are embracing the possibility of meeting their loved ones again, even if only in the virtual world. Might the Bosnian woman whom I talked about in chapter 2 who is unable to dream of her lost children find solace in meeting them in the online world? While some people might be thrilled by the new technological possibility of interacting with the avatars of those they have lost, others might find this horrifying. In both cases, loss remains loss, even if one fantasizes that it is not.

5

Love Is Blind

WHEN WE MAKE SOMEONE the object of our desire or we idealize them, ignorance often plays a part, which is why we are not wrong to say that love is blind. In the throes of a romantic embrace, seeing the other too clearly may endanger the fantasy, so lovers close their eyes to keep their passion alive. Nowadays, however, there appears to be a change in the way people deal with the self-delusion that love requires. People who search for a partner on the internet have to fill out lengthy questionnaires about the qualities they seek in a lover, as if it were possible to rationally describe what triggers our desire. Secret algorithms match them with potential partners, and in some cases, dating apps rate their users on their desirability, as if metrics can help people when they are navigating their way through the complicated paths of their own and others' desires. And when people do form relationships, it seems ever more difficult to keep the mystery alive with social media, mobile phones, and all kinds of surveillance apparatuses making it easy to track your lover's every thought and movement. But do people really want love to no longer be blind? And how is love connected to ignorance?

Love, Hate, and Ignorance

When Jacques Lacan spoke about love, he pointed out that in love, we give (or promise to give) what we do not have and we seek and see in others what they do not possess.[1] We create a fantasy to cover up the "lack" in the other, and when that fantasy collapses, we fall out of love or replace love with hate. As with love, hate also requires us to close our eyes; sometimes this allows us not to see the similarities between us and the object of our hatred, and sometimes it helps us to forget that we once loved that person. When we are falling out of love, we rarely start hating our partner straight away. Rather it is a gradual process by which the very thing that attracted us to that person in the first place becomes the one thing that annoys us, until eventually we can no longer tolerate it. When I was younger, I remember having coffee with a fellow student who suddenly started telling me how when he was falling in love with a woman, he would find the way the woman picked up a coffee cup and slowly brought it to her lips sublime. Listening to how she sipped her coffee and observing her gestures would incite strong desire in this young man. However, when he was falling out of love, the same gestures would become unbearable. He had the urge to close his eyes and put his hands over his ears, because what at the start of the romance had aroused desire incited only disgust by its end.

In his early work, Lacan placed ignorance as the third element in a triangle that includes love and hate and involves a conjunction of the symbolic, the imaginary, and the real.[2]

While love often idealizes the images of the other, it also involves symbolic recognition. A person, for example, may want to acknowledge his or her love by celebrating significant anniversaries, putting a love lock on a public bridge, or, the ultimate symbol of commitment, exchanging wedding rings. With hate, a quality or aspect of the other's appearance that might once have inspired affection may be used to demonize and dehumanize him or her. Social media are full of such images, unflattering and sometimes even monstrous-looking photographs of politicians or celebrities who have become unpopular for one reason or another.

Love and hate focus on what is ungraspable in a person, and no matter the words or images we use to try to encapsulate it, we fail. There is often no rational reason why one person should love or hate another, and that is because both emotions rely on ignorance. Neither can exist without strategies that enable the person who loves or hates to avoid knowing too much about the object of his or her emotions. Ignorance, in terms of ignoring and being ignored, also plays a role. While some (as we will discover with the incels in chapter 6) feel anger and animosity toward those they feel ignored by, for others their feelings of love only get stronger when the other does not pay attention to them. As French psychoanalyst Michel Silvestre astutely observes, people in love often do not necessarily want to hear back from the object of their attraction: "From the times men write about love, it is clear that they survived far better the longer the beauty remained mute, the longer she did not answer at all."[3]

While love may turn into hate, a reversal when hate turns into love is also possible. Ignorance plays a vital role in this reversal, as it allows lovers to forget or ignore what originally incited their hate and suddenly start looking at the other with fresh eyes. It is as if they see a new "truth" that causes them to switch from hate to love.

The way that love can transform into hate or hate to love is the central theme of Daphne du Maurier's novel *My Cousin*

Rachel.[4] The lead character is Phillip, an orphan who was raised by his loving and affectionate older cousin Ambrose. When Phillip is in his twenties, Ambrose falls ill, and doctors advise him to spend time abroad to avoid the cold British winter. In Florence, Ambrose falls in love with the beautiful and mysterious Rachel, and they soon marry. Ambrose's letters to Phillip are at first full of admiration for Rachel. In time, however, there are hints that all is not well in their marriage. When Phillip receives Ambrose's last letter, he notices that it is written in a shaky hand. Ambrose writes about his illness, accuses Rachel of trying to poison him, and urges Phillip to come to Italy as quickly as possible, saying, "She has done for me last, Rachel, my torment."[5] Phillip arrives too late to save his cousin. And Rachel has disappeared.

Back home, Phillip learns that he has inherited his cousin's estate, and when Rachel announces that she is planning to visit, he fantasizes about avenging Ambrose, for whose death he blames her. Slowly, however, he becomes infatuated with Rachel and starts to ignore the many clues that suggest she did kill Ambrose. Phillip showers Rachel with money and gifts and, against all advice, decides to bequeath the estate to her, hoping that she will marry him and that they will enjoy the inheritance together.

The story illustrates perfectly the blindness of love. Philip is like a man bewitched who cannot see anything but the object of his passion. His anger toward Rachel and his desire to avenge the death of his beloved cousin are, over time, transformed into total adoration. Under the self-deluded pretext that he is honoring Ambrose's love for Rachel, he disregards the warnings in Ambrose's letters. At one point he even decides to hide Ambrose's last letter under a stone in the woods, as if anything that might intrude into his lover's fantasy must be physically removed from his life. Similarly, he ignores Rachel's increasing coldness, her excessive spending habits, and her secret ties to an Italian friend.

After many twists and turns during which Phillip fears she is trying to poison him, Rachel ends up dying in an accident. He is bereft and will for the rest of his life remain uncertain about the woman he hated and loved in equal measure: Was she truly a murderess, or had he misjudged her?

In this novel, we see hate, love, and ignorance at play in the relationship between the two main protagonists. At first we see from a distance Ambrose's love for Rachel slowly change to hate, a hate that Phillip accepts and adopts, even though he does not know the facts, because she has taken away his beloved cousin. When he in turn falls in love with her, ignorance also is an essential factor, acting as an intermediary between hate and love. All of his feelings of hate are pushed away and no amount of information will make Phillip distrust or stop loving Rachel. Knowledge and truth become unimportant, ignored, or denied when in the throes of lust or love.

Love and Lies

Shakespeare wrote many lines about love and blindness. In one sonnet, he asks,

> Thou blind fool, Love, what dost thou to mine eyes
> That they behold, and see not what they see?[6]

In another, he observes,

> When my love swears that she is made of truth,
> I do believe her, though I know she lies.[7]

Believing here takes precedence over knowing. While belief and knowledge can coexist, knowledge is often pushed aside, so that the lover can preserve the fantasy that keeps love alive.

Believing in lies or ignoring the truth is so much an accepted part of love relationships that people who cheat on their partners are often advised to keep denying their actions for as long as possible. Sometimes a strong capacity for ignorance and denial allows partners to mend their relationship. Such was the case with a couple I will call Anna and Mike. Mike was a pilot and thus often away from home. Anna once, by chance, stumbled upon an exchange of email love letters between Mike and a young flight attendant. When she confronted Mike with her discovery, he at first claimed that he knew nothing about the messages. When Anna showed her husband the emails, he made up a story that his colleagues must have broken into his email account and created the flirty love notes as a joke. Although Anna was at first rightly suspicious of this story, she soon came to believe it and focused her anger on the irresponsible colleagues who had almost ruined her marriage. In this example, the denial of the cheating partner allowed the other partner to embrace a particular type of belief that allowed her to stay in her marriage—another version of Lacan's idea of the passion for ignorance at work. It is not so much that she ignored the truth; rather, she clung with passion to the story that her husband invented, as it enabled her to stay with him and keep the life they had together.

Sometimes, however, an admission of "truth" can be a way to keep a partner in the dark about one's behavior. This happened in a marriage where a wife felt that something was amiss in her relationship with her husband. The latter was away from home a lot and, when he was there, would spend much of his

time sending texts he was careful to conceal. Once, when the
wife managed to see her husband's phone, she discovered a series of messages from him to an unknown woman. The husband
appeared shocked by her discovery but did not try to deny the
texts. Instead, he promised to stop seeing the other woman. The
wife was happy, the husband was pleased that she had been ap-
peased, and things seemed to slowly go back to normal in their
marriage. It eventually came to light that the other woman with
whom he was supposedly texting was an invention he had created in order to cover up the fact that he was actually having an
affair with another man. Here, a token "truth" was created to
maintain a partner's ignorance. The man wanted to keep the
symbolic pact, his marriage, alive, as a charade to mask the truth
of his affair with his male lover.

Fantasy shapes a person's perception of reality; as a result,
that fantasy rarely changes when that person discovers new
knowledge, truth, or facts. This is mainly because fantasy has
little to do with how things are in the "real world." Often, the
subject's fantasy acts as a defense against "reality testing," as well
as against interpretations that might undermine it.[8] As a result,
no amount of truth or information about the object of one's
love can change the lover's perceptions.

Who Am I for the Other?

Denial and ignorance are often at work when a person wants a
relationship to succeed and does everything possible to keep
alive the fantasy that sustains it. However, in some cases of willful ignorance, we are not dealing with a person closing his or
her eyes or imagining something that did not happen; instead,
we have a person knowing that something is not true and at the
same time pretending that it is.

This happened to a girl I will call Maya who, at the tender age of ten, lost her mother to cancer. On her birthday, for several years after her mother died, Maya's father would give her a letter supposedly written by her mother before she died. The letter was full of praise for how well Maya was doing, what a lovely young girl she was, and how proud her mother would have been had she been able to celebrate the birthday with her. Maya regarded each of these letters as the most precious present she could ever receive. I was deeply moved when Maya showed me these treasures and wondered how many more letters her father had kept for her. So I was shocked when he told me not only that he had written the letters himself but also that Maya was perfectly aware of this fact. The truth was that Maya's mother had not wanted to burden her daughter with such letters beyond the grave and had wanted her to go on living her life without being haunted by messages from her deceased mother. However, when Maya's first birthday passed without her mother, she kept asking her father what her mother would have wished for her on her birthday and whether she left any letters before she died. Since there was no actual letter left to be opened at the time of Maya's birthday, the father proposed that he write a letter and that they both pretend that it was from her mother. Maya was delighted by this arrangement and was overjoyed when a new letter arrived for her on each subsequent birthday. While Maya knew very well that her father wrote the letters, she lived in willed ignorance of this fact. The letters opened a space for her in which she could imagine that her mother was speaking to her, even if it came from her father's pen. While this little girl could remember her mother's love, she craved symbolic proof of it. The fake letters played the role of a symbolic sign of the fact that she was the object of her late mother's love. The father, as the writer of these letters, acted as an intermediary, as someone who attested to this love, and the letters became almost like a perpetually renewed contract that made maternal love exist. In *My Cousin Rachel*, Phillip needs to hide Ambrose's letter so that his love for Rachel is not challenged; in the case of Maya, a fake letter expresses maternal—and paternal—love.

To the question, What do I mean to another? we invent an answer that in some cases can be gratifying and life affirming but in others may open the door to self-destruction. Gilead Nachmani describes the case of an eleven-year-old boy who was sent to psychoanalysis for traumas related to the fact that his father had gone to his office in the morning three months beforehand and never come back.[9] After this traumatic event, the word "daddy" was never spoken in the house and the missing man was only referred to formally as "father." It was as if his absence had changed his symbolic status, and the term "daddy" could only be used for a person who was present and "father" for one who was absent.

The boy was deeply affected by his father's disappearance. He started playing truant from school, he was unruly at home, and his mother stopped showing him affection and in general ignored him. It was as if in her grief, she was unable to see that her son was also suffering and his very presence in the house annoyed her.

At some point, she decided that her son needed therapy, but as the analyst noted, she did not bother to accompany her son to their first session, presumably because she was too busy. The analyst noticed that the boy was dressed in clothes that were too big for him and looked as though they might have belonged to the father. The boy's posture resembled that of an old man: he was slouching, and he looked exhausted and dragged his feet.

The boy talked about his father's disappearance in a detached and emotionless way, but on an unconscious level, he deeply identified with his father. His truancy from school was like a reenactment of his father's disappearance, and by dressing in his father's clothes and walking like an old man, he was trying to embody the absent parent. To begin with, he showed signs of depression, but soon he also expressed anxiety and feelings of guilt. He found it increasingly difficult to distinguish fantasy from reality. His father had often worked long hours, and the boy, resenting the fact that his father was rarely at home, had often fantasized that his father might fall ill and be forced to stay home more. When his father disappeared, the boy became worried that such wishes had been granted and that he had caused his father's disappearance.

As the analyst concluded, "Essentially, he began his therapy as a self-convicted felon. Although his sense of guilt was specific, he acknowledged it mostly by denial, and by his insistent commitment to having 'no needs.' He boasted of not needing anyone, of being rugged and definitely independent. He needed no one."[10]

An interesting moment during psychoanalysis occurred when the analyst noticed the boy had been secretly stealing food from the analyst's fridge. The analyst realized that the boy's mother had forgotten to feed her son. When the analyst asked her to explain, she admitted that not feeding her son was a way of punishing him for her husband's disappearance. She, too, was secretly blaming the boy for what had happened, since she often felt that her husband loved his son more than her.

While we do not learn from the analyst's account how the analysis of the boy proceeded or whether the father was finally found, we can detect in this story several types of denial that play essential roles in interpersonal relationships. First, the father's disappearance (if actually intentional or imagined as intentional) can be understood as a powerful form of disregard for his family: he physically removed himself from all sight and contact with them. He ignored them and thus rejected them. Second, by not talking to her son and by insisting on using the word "father," the mother declined to address what had happened and, at the same time, denied the emotional links between the boy and his "daddy." Third, the mother and son ignored—and even punished—each other in their suffering. The mother stopped noticing the boy to the point of not feeding him. The boy "ignored" his mother when "disappearing" from school and the family home.

Amid all this drama, where the truth about the father's disappearance was ignored and where mother and son ignored each other's feelings, the boy sought recognition and love. By transgressing the rules at home, not going to school, dressing in his father's clothes, and even stealing food from his analyst, he was in his way calling for help, and he luckily found it in his analyst.

Ignoring and being ignored are clearly a vital part of all kinds of love and relationships, including our relationship with ourselves. Psychoanalyst Ruth Imber describes the case of Anna, who felt that she was always ignored and was searching for a cure for various maladies by going from doctor to doctor.[11] While she was trying to get attention and craved finding a medical professional who would recognize her suffering and help alleviate her pain, she prevented this from happening by continually changing doctors. When Anna was dissatisfied with traditional medicine, she began sampling alternative therapies, trying everything from homoeopaths and acupuncturists to diet specialists. Exhausted by this search for help, she ended up in psychoanalysis, hoping for a solution to her suffering while again doing everything to sabotage the process of change she actually needed.

In the course of her sessions, Anna complained about being ignored in many areas of her life. When her husband's brother and his wife became parents, she felt that they started ignoring her. Her feelings of jealousy and envy were, however, not only directed at her extended family but also related to her position in society. As an immigrant, she felt that she had been ignored and deprived since childhood and was angry that her mother had a disability, which she thought could have been prevented if they had not lived in such unfortunate circumstances in her country of origin. In addition, just before her mother died, she also learned that she was not her mother's biological daughter.

In therapy it became clear that Anna had always been afraid of loss and attachment, and that she had dealt with her anxiety by never putting all her eggs in one basket. Going from doctor to doctor and from one therapist to another was part of a strategy for preventing abandonment. In her desire to appease her anxiety and not feel rejected, this woman was always the first to abandon a relationship. In the end, she also quit her analysis.

This case illustrates how a subject often finds a particular painful enjoyment (*jouissance*) in suffering. While claiming that she was searching for knowledge that would help her change her life, Anna did everything to avoid and ignore it. Although she did finally offer important information in analysis about the loss of her biological mother, she decided not to go further in exploring the relationship between this fact and her fear of abandonment and, by ignoring this important fact about herself, compounded the feeling of being ignored, which contributed to her unhappiness and lack of self-love.

New Forms of Ignorance in Love

In online dating, image plays a powerful role. In their dating profiles, people often use images of themselves that have been significantly altered or old photos that make them look younger and more attractive. Given that online dating platforms focus primarily on looks, it is hardly surprising that people are incentivized to lie and present misleading and idealized images of themselves. Equally important to the way these platforms work are the deceptions and ignorance related to people's desires. People are encouraged to think there are set criteria they can stipulate that are guaranteed to help them find their desired potential partner. Relying on these self-stated criteria, online dating sites match people with the help of algorithms, which create their own types of ignorance. Dating sites that allow users to filter matches by race could be argued to reinforce racial bias, and those that generate recommendations on the basis of "collaborative filtering," where people are sent profiles of potential matches on the basis of what other users are choosing, are further disadvantaging those whose profiles are less popular.[12] Research into how dating sites work has shown that the suggestions people receive through the workings of the algorithms significantly affect users' behavior. If a dating site predicts that two people are incompatible, they are likely to have a less successful interaction than when they are predicted to be compatible. So in many cases, rather than helping people find a good match, they are often limiting their options. Researchers of online dating have also observed that people's desires are unconscious, and while they may be influenced by what is presented to them, they can be even more excited by the unexpected.[13] While the algorithms on conventional dating sites make surprising but positive encounters hard to experience, they are even more unlikely on dating sites like Chemistry, which use pseudo-psychological testing to predict how compatible one's hormones and neurotransmitters will be with potential partners.

If algorithms on dating apps are trying to predict people's desires, a new class of apps hopes to make it easier for people to understand each other's romantic intentions by using artificial intelligence to analyze people's text messages.[14] This is designed to give people the sense that they can predict and control their own and other's emotions, even if this does not reflect reality. In addition to the apps that are supposed to make love easier to find, there are self-help gurus who teach people how to feign ignorance in order to attract love, how not to appear overeager, and how to keep one's emotions in check when pursuing a potential partner. As we will see in the next chapter in the case of pickup artists, ignorance and self-mastery are often cherished as the ultimate skills a lover needs to perfect.

Yet despite all the apps, the self-help advice, and the multiple ways of communicating, relationships are not becoming easier, perhaps partly because of this emphasis on ignoring others as a means of emotional control. One obvious example is "ghosting," which is a relatively recent phenomenon associated with the new technologies. It occurs when a personal relationship is ended when one person suddenly, without explanation, withdraws all communication. Phone calls are not answered, text messages are not replied to, and the person who is being ghosted has no idea why. They are powerless, rejected, and ignored. The person who is doing the ghosting, in contrast, not only has control but also has very powerfully expressed his or her indifference to the other person's feelings.

Tinder and similar dating apps have a form of indifference built into their design. One can quickly swipe out of sight a person one is not interested in. Behind this simple mechanism of swiping lies an elaborate algorithm that gives each user his or her own "desirability" score and then presents possible matches based on that score. Just as a computer gamer gets more points if he or she plays with a person with a higher score, a Tinder dater's "desirability" score increases if he or she is matched with people with higher ratings. A journalist who had been using Tinder started exploring how this secret ranking system works. He asked Tinder to show him his personal score. He expected that he would be among the most desirable men on Tinder and was disappointed when he learned that his ranking was only on the "upper end of the average."[15] In the end he wished he had not found out his score, as it did not exactly boost his ego.[16]

Tinder and similar online dating sites are opening up new dilemmas over old questions about what kind of an object of desire one might be for others. As French psychoanalyst Clotilde Leguil points out, these dating sites are becoming "sites of demand."[17] People demand something (recognition, love, approval) that fulfills their conscious and unconscious desires from others they do not know, but when they do not receive what they are looking for from their anonymous interlocutors, anger and disappointment kick in.

Since falling in love with other humans is so complex and difficult, it is not surprising that in the developed world one finds an increase of emotional attachment to inanimate objects. For some, sex robots are replacing human partners; for others, computer avatars offer enjoyable companionship. Even old-fashioned statues can provoke strong attachment.

This was demonstrated at the end of Antony Gormley's 2007 show *Event Horizon* in London. After statues had stood for three months on the roofs of buildings, been hung from bridges, or popped up in other unexpected public spaces, people started worrying what would happen to the figures when the show ended. They asked, Will the statues lie forgotten in some godforsaken warehouse? Will they be destroyed? Will they be used in other settings? Those who worried the most about the destinies of Gormley's sculptures found solace in writing scenarios on various blogs in which they imagined the best possible future for them. Often, these bloggers' proposals stressed that the statues must be kept together—perhaps in a park or a gallery. The Austrian artist Peter Arlt approached similar anxieties about the loneliness of statues in the late 1990s when he decided to unite for only one day the historical statues of the saints, which are placed on bridges in Austria. Arlt went to great lengths to secure permissions from various state organizations so that some statues were able to meet each other at one particular public space, albeit briefly.

How can statues provoke such strong emotions? Why did some people experience anxiety over the statues in Gormley's *Event Horizon* project and their imagined future loneliness? In today's highly individualized society, where loneliness is on the rise, it might be that for some a discussion about lonely statues provides a way to project their painful feelings onto a material object. Nevertheless, when they engaged with others to figure out how to prevent the statutes from being abandoned, they took the first steps toward exiting their solitude.

The turn to loving inanimate objects may help people who struggle with the feeling that they are ignored. For some, a robot truly might be a solution to loneliness.

Writers Danielle Knafo and Rocco Lo Bosco have interviewed people who love plastic dolls and who frequent the iDollator online community. A man called Davecat confessed that his dolls are a form of comfort because they are "beautiful, nonjudgmental people that will always be there when [he] come[s] home."[18] For this man, losing a doll would feel like "losing a limb." Yet while he claims to be content with his quiet life at home with his dolls, he complains that he cannot talk with his friends about his passion because he is afraid other people will not understand his attachment and will judge him harshly. The fundamental questions of "What do I mean to other people?" and "How do others see me?" keep haunting people even when they have replaced human companionship with that of dolls or robots.

While some may derive satisfaction from their relationships with dolls or robots, the designers of robots know that people's attraction to their creations can be accentuated if the latter appear not too interested in humans. In 2012, a robotic doll that looked like an elegant young lady was placed in a Tokyo department store. She was sitting in a chair "staring at her smart phone and mostly ignoring the thousand visitors" who came to look at her. The doll showed a range of emotions as if she were reacting to texts on her phone, but occasionally she looked up at her onlookers and smiled. Hiroshi Ishiguro, the engineer who created this robot, believes that human emotions like romantic love are nothing but responses to stimuli and thus can be manipulated. He hopes that perfecting pneumatic joints, gently moving the arch of the doll's mechanical brow, and making her show a range of subtle facial expressions may result in her forming "a perfectly engineered bond with us."[19] Ishiguro wants people who are observing his doll look at her smartphone to imagine she is reading their messages, to project their feelings onto her, creating a bond with her, even falling in love. However, one can imagine that even with a perfectly designed robot, people's unconscious fantasies will remain something that cannot ever be fully provoked and controlled.

6

The Fear of Being Ignored

FROM INCEL TO IMPOSTOR

IN *THE PICTURE OF DORIAN GRAY*, Oscar Wilde remarks, "There is only one thing in the world worse than being talked about, and that is not being talked about." In these times of incessant surveillance, when many feel they are constantly being watched and controlled, there are still some people who worry that they are not being acknowledged by particular groups or that they are being ignored by society as a whole. It is certainly true that postindustrial society, with its emphasis on individualism and worship of celebrity, coupled with the prevalence of social media, has increased the pressure on individuals to make themselves visible. There is overwhelming emphasis on the need to stand out from the crowd, excel at self-promotion, and receive recognition from others in the form of online likes and shares of their posts. The ultimate expression of this professionalization of the personal is the emergence of the social media influencer, who uses his or her profile and authority online to influence others, and a vast advice and work-related coaching industry that not only focuses on making a person more productive but also encourages the manipulation of others and teaches people how to pursue their goals ruthlessly.

Nowadays we are free to create for ourselves an image or public persona that is attractive to others and makes us feel good. But the downside of being able to create one's own image is the pressure to achieve a level of airbrushed perfectionism, to conform to an ideal, and then the inevitable dissatisfaction and deep anxiety about how one might be judged by others if one fails to live up to that ideal. This disjuncture between image and reality can lead people to fear being "found out." Conversely, if people do not receive positive feedback for the personas they create and are not liked or followed, they can feel ignored by and even angry toward a world that seems to recognize and validate everyone but them. These dilemmas can be illustrated by comparing people who suffer from impostor syndrome with men who identify with the so-called incel (involuntary celibate) movement. In both cases, these are relatively new phenomena that capture something fundamental about how a person is recognized or not recognized by others.

In modern society people are encouraged to nurture entirely unrealistic ideas of what they should look like, the relationships they should have, and the kind of lifestyle they should aspire to, and as a result, when they fail to live up to these ideals, many feel that they are substandard, slighted, and ignored. People now exist in a much expanded social setting compared with the past, when their social interactions were limited to the people they could physically interact with in real time. This is no longer the case thanks to social media, and the very different nature of virtual interactions and recognition have changed the sense people have of themselves, and of whether they feel acknowledged or ignored.

The New Mirror

Small children do not recognize themselves in the reflection that they see in a mirror. They do not even recognize their reflection as an image but instead think it is another child. Self-recognition does not happen naturally or spontaneously. Language, culture, and especially other people are essential for this recognition to occur. Usually, the person to whom a child is most attached explains that the image in the mirror corresponds to the child himself or herself. "Baby, that is you!" the mother might say, pointing to the image in the mirror. But the child will have a hard time connecting this image to his or her self-perception. The clumsy, vulnerable body of the child does not seem to go with the solid, contained reflection that appears in the mirror.

In modern society, the changes I have already discussed in how people perceive themselves have led some people to experience increasing difficulties in recognizing themselves in the mirror—in some cases quite literally. Japanese psychoanalyst Daisuke Fukuda reported on a client who suffered from anxiety in front of her reflection in the mirror. The woman had the urge to break every mirror in her vicinity. By destroying the reflective surface, she hoped to alleviate the anxiety that she felt when she observed her own image.[1]

While this condition, known as eisoptrophobia, is not new, one wonders how the occurrence of such a painful response is linked to the changes that have occurred over the last few decades. In recent years, Japan, along with every other capitalist society, has experienced significant growth in its beauty industry. In most public places, Japanese girls and women, just like women in most other countries, are overwhelmed with advertisements presenting images of female beauty to compare themselves with and aspire to.

While one cannot link such profound psychological expressions of anxiety over appearance directly to culture or ideology or claim that all women are breaking mirrors or trying to change their bodies for exactly the same reasons, it is the case that culture has some influence, as we shall see shortly. And perhaps the barrage of idealized images that women are subject to nowadays affects them even if the symptoms that express their anxiety develop in unique and individualized ways.

From our early childhood, the way we see ourselves in the mirror is influenced by others around us and by culture in general. When social perceptions of the body change, we start regarding ourselves in different ways. Susie Orbach, in her book *Bodies*, shows how we perceive nakedness, weight, and beauty differently if we live in different cultural settings. However, she also points out that these settings can mark us in an unconscious way, which is why a person who in his or her early childhood was brought up with a particular attitude toward the body might have difficulty changing when he or she starts living in a different social context.[2]

Instagram, Facebook, and other social media have created an online mirror stage that has led to new problems of self-recognition. In addition to the pressure to constantly promote oneself like a brand and always present the best version of oneself to the world, people are obliged to recognize others in their mutual pursuit of social visibility. Liking and sharing posts by other people has become the new price of friendship, and there is an expectation of being liked and recognized back. When you like and recognize others and they ignore you, it causes considerable psychological distress, and in extreme instances this distress can lead to deep anger and acts of violence, as in the case of the incels.[3]

Ignored "Beta Men"

The dissatisfaction of those who have in some way "made it" on the ladder of social recognition and of those who feel that they have not, paradoxically, follow similar patterns of self-criticism, often coupled with aggression—either toward oneself or toward others. In the context of a climate of heightened individualism, the economization of life, and the glorification of success, ignoring a person can be seen as an act of aggression in itself, which may well generate an aggressive response from the one who has been ignored. In many cases of violence carried out by so-called lone wolves, one hears that the perpetrators felt ignored and saw their violence as a way of simultaneously seeking revenge against those who ignored them and gaining the attention they craved. Some attackers post YouTube videos or manifestos in the hope of leaving their mark. Quite often, the attackers use social media to inform the public that they will not endure being endlessly ignored and that they consider taking the lives of innocent victims, and even their own, a price worth paying to finally get the attention they have craved for so long. French psychoanalyst Fethi Benslama, in his analysis of terrorism, urged the French media not to publish images of terrorists after they had perpetrated attacks, since such recognition and publicity might encourage others to commit similar crimes to gain attention.[4]

The internet offers a special kind of recognition to people who claim that they are ignored, whether for political or personal reasons. An example of extreme behavior arising from a feeling of being ignored is that of those men who identify as incels and claim that desirable women ignore them, so they are unable to have sex. They are involuntarily celibate, as they have not chosen celibacy but have had it forced on them because they have been overlooked by a society that cherishes particular ideals of success and attractiveness. Incels call men who have success with women because of their good looks and accomplishments "Chads" and women who are beautiful and tick the other attributes of desirability "Stacys." Those women who do not look hyperfeminine and are thus perceived by incels as less attractive are called "Beckys."

Incels believe that particular biological features make men attractive to women: "Chins and jaws, the most enhanced facial features in the millimeters of bone meme, are particular obsessions of many incel communities, as members believe women are biologically drawn to men with prominent ones, while guys with weak chins and slight overbites are doomed to lives of solitude."[5] The idealized Chad is the all-powerful man, and incels write about him with a mixture of admiration and disgust. He is an alpha male, muscular, good looking, successful. Desirable women, the so-called Stacys, are irresistibly drawn to this kind of man and do not even notice incels, who are "beta men." These rants against alpha men allegedly preventing incels from having sex are strangely reminiscent of Sigmund Freud's myth of a primal horde where the sons complain that they have no access to women because of a powerful primal father figure who takes all the women for himself.[6] In Freud's story, after the men kill the primal father, they do not find enjoyment but rather are haunted by feelings of guilt. With incels aggression is often directed against women, but the feeling of guilt related to actual or imagined violence against women seems to be lacking.

In online forums where incels express their anger at not being able to have sex, there are disturbingly graphic descriptions of how men might punish women who ignore them. Incels' ideas of how to make women notice them range from fantasies of gang rape to advice on how to follow women in public without being cautioned or arrested. The thrill of following a woman is linked to the fact that at some point the woman will have to notice the man who is pursuing her.

The cruel fantasies of how to get attention from desirable women played out in the incels' online community reflect a desire to humiliate and scare women who in real life do not respond favorably to their advances. The fantasies of stalking a woman or gang-raping her express a perverted desire for recognition that is reminiscent of the real-life rapes that occurred during the war in Bosnia in the 1990s. Serbian soldiers often raped Bosnian women, insisting that the woman's father or husband remain present so that they would be humiliated by their own impotence and inability to prevent the attack on their loved one.[7]

While the majority of incels confine their enjoyment of such fantasies to online platforms, in recent years a few have committed acts of extreme and murderous violence in public spaces. The most well known is the case of Elliot Rodger, who killed six people and wounded fourteen others near the University of California, Santa Barbara, campus in 2014. In the course of his killing spree, Rodger uploaded a film called "Elliot Rodger's Retribution" onto his YouTube channel and emailed a manifesto in which he described his desire to fit in and be recognized. Although he came from a privileged background, Rodger claimed that he had felt rejected throughout his life because women were incapable of seeing value in him and he never felt cool enough. As a result of feeling ignored by them, he decided to launch a "war on women." The idea was to target the most attractive women on campus, members of a prestigious sorority that for Rodger represented everything he hated (and desired) in women. They were blond, beautiful, spoiled, heartless, wicked "bitches" whom he wanted to punish and, by doing so, show that he was superior, a true alpha male. Rodger killed himself just as he was about to be caught by police.

After his death, Rodger was hailed by many incels as a hero, and some imitated him with their own acts of violence. In the spring of 2018, Alek Minassian drove a rental van onto a crowded Toronto city sidewalk, killing ten people and wounding fourteen. Minassian announced his attack by writing an online tribute to Elliot Rodger and saying, "The Incel Rebellion has already begun! We will overthrow all the Chads and Stacys! All hail the Supreme Gentleman Elliot Rodger!" In the fall of 2018, at a yoga studio in Tallahassee, another self-identified incel, Scott P. Beierle, shot two people and injured five.

Sympathizers with the incel movement have suggested that the violence could have been avoided if there had been some women willing to have sex with these men.[8] This is clearly a ridiculous statement, and the term "incel" is in itself a misnomer, since the most active members of these online communities do not seem to be actively searching for women with whom they might be able to have relationships. Rather they take a particular pleasure in finding ever more obstacles for not engaging with members of the opposite sex and at the same time ranting about how unfair it is that women ignore them. Incels also subscribe to an unrealistic ideal of the kind of woman with whom they would like to have sex: they do not want to have sex with any woman but only those who have not had sex before because they cannot tolerate the thought that their potential partners might be able to compare them with anyone else or might have any options but to be with them.

While incels rant against Stacys for only paying attention to alpha men, they desire and despise them at the same time for being, according to the incel stereotype, attractive, spoiled, successful, and promiscuous all at once. The contempt for their alleged limitless promiscuity is also fueled by their unavailability. This alleged promiscuity and unavailability leads the incels to create a fantasy of a woman who is both a virgin and available to them but no one else, a woman who will belong to one man only and has never belonged to another—a patriarchal ideal born of ignorance and hate, which sees women as possessions with no will or freedom of their own and which reflects the dangers of feeling ignored and ignoring the reality of others.

The Game of Ignorance

The majority of men who feel ignored by women do not resort to such extreme measures and turn instead to the considerable amounts of advice offered by the seduction industry, which claims that it can instruct men how to get women's attention in order to have sex with them. Ignorance plays a vital role in seduction techniques as a form of manipulation and as a strategy to arouse a woman's interest and desire.

In *The Game* by Neil Strauss, which has a cult status in the seduction industry, and on various pickup artists' online forums, one can find scenarios outlining how a man can use active ignoring or disregarding tactics to his advantage.[9] A man who is chatting with two women and is interested in the more attractive of the pair is told to pay excessive attention to the less attractive one and ignore the one who is used to being the object of attention. This is supposed to provoke interest in the more attractive woman so she will start to wonder why he is ignoring her. A man in a bar who notices an attractive woman on her own is advised to mix ignorance with slight criticism. When he has the chance to approach the woman, he is supposed to say something positive, like, "What a lovely dress you are wearing. The color accentuates your beautiful eyes." The woman might smile and thank the man for the compliment, but will probably not pay too much attention to him. At which point, the man is supposed to surprise the woman with a slight criticism, like, "Too bad, your haircut doesn't do you any favors." After delivering this criticism, the man is supposed to turn away and feign disregard. According to pickup artist theory, many women will be provoked and look for an opportunity to come back to the man and ask him what he meant by his remark. According to common sense, many women will either ignore the pickup artist completely or tell him where to go.

This kind of advice tries to put into action the Lacanian theory that the desire of the Other often provokes desire in the woman and that an essential part of this process is the woman asking herself, "Who am I for the Other? How do others see me? What kind of an object am I?" Because she desires an explanation of the man's comments, the woman will put the man in the position of a master, one who is supposed to know certain things. It is not that the woman at this point starts desiring the man, but she becomes uncertain enough about herself to start paying him attention.

The seduction industry relies on the premises of capitalism and ideas of choice, self-improvement, and continuous work. While strategies of seduction are nothing new and history is full of manuals that try to help members of both sexes appear more attractive to each other, the contemporary seduction movement has created a whole industry that relies on coaches, heavily promoted books, courses, boot camps, and videos testifying to the success of certain seduction techniques. The idea behind this lucrative business is that any man can learn how to get a woman if only he works hard enough to learn the appropriate techniques and invests time in practicing them.

Seduction is a choice, as is the appearance and condition of one's body, one's wealth, and other tokens of success.

The seduction industry presents sex as something that can be achieved if one follows the right strategy, using the tricks of a skilled pickup artist who knows how to score with women. In her critique of this industry, Rachel O'Neill rightly points out that it substitutes sexuality and desire for the logic of assessment, surveillance, and control, and although it adopts the pretense of artistry, it actually mimics the advertising industry in its manipulation of emotion and "offers up a system of rules and interdictions by which sex and relationships can be managed rather than experienced."[10] O'Neill also observes that many of the seduction techniques used resemble techniques sales people use to score a deal. Some men who have attended seduction seminars later claim that while they might not have found a partner, other domains of their lives dramatically improved after they learned to be more assertive and better at presenting themselves. Many who go to such seminars continuously "train" to maintain their skills since they are afraid that a moment of inaction might result in them losing their newfound powers.

This, then, is a version of the "art of the deal" in which women are the object. Often they are dropped as quickly as they are "scored" so that the man can pursue another woman whom he sees as being harder to get and thus more desirable. Many advocates of these contemporary seduction practices are continuously going through the motions of picking up women and dumping them so that they can reassure themselves of their mastery. Men who go from one hookup to another do not seem to get enjoyment from the sex as such, but rather from being successful in applying their pickup techniques and being recognized and desired. They believe that having sex with as many women as possible while they still can will satisfy them when they are old and are ignored by the women they find attractive. The reality, however, is that they are often consumed with deep anxiety and obsessed with their performance, learning new tricks, constantly evolving their technique, and expanding their list of conquests. A pickup artist is thus a version of a contemporary worker. He is selling himself, getting better and better results, and his payment is a growing number of notches on the bedpost. One can easily imagine him collecting other symbols of success—climbing the ladder in a computer game, collecting points as a consumer, or increasing his number of likes and followers in social media.

What lurks behind incel discourse is the idea that being ignored by women directly causes the men's frustration and leads them to react with aggression in an attempt to take control of their relationship with women. If a woman won't willingly interact with him, the incel will force her to on his own terms. In the seduction industry, this hostility is subtly molded into pickup techniques that trick women into having sex by manipulating their emotions and their desires. Success comes from manipulation and by ignoring the feelings and desires of the women involved and only recognizing the desires of the men.

Impostor Syndrome

Two key exhortations of neoliberal ideology are "Everyone can make it" and "Fake it until you make it." Achieving success requires you to look successful or pretend that success is on its way. Numerous coaches teach people how to dress, behave, and talk in order to give the appearance of success. In a time when success has been raised to an ideal, it is not surprising that a new syndrome has emerged—so-called impostor syndrome. While the traditional meaning of the term "impostor" applies to people who deliberately present themselves as someone else, impostor syndrome refers to people who feel that they do not deserve the symbolic role others attribute to them. Helene Deutsch links the idea of the impostor to child's play since playing allows children temporarily to take on other roles. When adults present themselves as someone else, there may be a combination of motives: financial gain, social status, the fulfillment of a fantasy about oneself, or an escape from the real world or internalized pressures. Equally, the steps taken by the impostor may vary—while some people take the name of someone else, others fraudulently take on symbolic insignias (diplomas or military decorations) or boast of achievements they have not accomplished. Deutsch believed the reason for doing this lay in the impostor's ego. The impostor often feels devalued and guilt ridden; hence "he needs to usurp the name of an individual who fulfills the requirements of his own magnificent ego ideal."[11] The problem of the guilt-ridden ego is also at work in the term "impostor syndrome" or "impostor phenomenon," which came into the public domain in the late 1970s when the psychologists Pauline R. Clance and Suzanne A. Imes wrote about high-achieving women who felt that they would be found out, that others would somehow "see" through them and recognize them as frauds.[12] Certain women also suffer from the perception that their success is the result of pure luck and that consequently they do not deserve public admiration. If at first this new syndrome seemed to apply mostly to women, in time men started suffering from it, too.

While traditional impostors pretended to be someone else so that they could come closer to an ideal, the new type of impostor seems to have come close to social ideals of success, but his or her self-perception is different from how others presumably perceive the person.

With both types of impostors, the issue is how a person perceives him- or herself regarding the Lacanian Big Other, the symbolic order in which he or she lives. If the first meaning of the term "impostor" involves a person fraudulently taking on the symbolic role of another or taking an identity without authorization, the second meaning of the term involves a perception that one is not up to the symbolic role one is inhabiting—that one is a fraud. While the first type of impostor wants to be someone else, the second worries that he or she is not the person others see. Both, however, have a problem with the fact that there is no such thing as a stable ego, that one never can fully embody an ego ideal, and that, as previous chapters have shown, one can never satisfactorily answer the question of what one's place in the world is or whether one is properly acknowledged by others.

While anxiety over how others regard us is nothing new, it seems to be amplified in times when one's image appears to be a matter of choice, something that can be manipulated or shaped, which is why the desire to look like someone else—that is, to become a "visual" impostor—has never been greater. As early as 1970, the neurologist MacDonald Critchley wrote about self-portraits as being a form of imposture, as artists often paint images of themselves that do not resemble the way they actually look.[13] With this observation Critchley hinted at a third meaning of the term, which has to do with people presenting themselves in images that do not match their actual appearance. In this way of thinking, self-portraiture would be a predecessor of today's selfies, which are increasingly staged or airbrushed images that bear little resemblance to how a person looks in real life.[14]

In contrast to people who are trying to look like someone else or who manipulate their image to be more favorably recognized by others, people who are afraid that they will be found out and that they are not who they appear to be do not complain about being ignored. Instead, they fear that they may be recognized too much—for example, that they will receive a promotion that they do not deserve. In times when so many complain that they are not recognized, this impostor anxiety, which is very painful for the afflicted individual, could turn out to be liberating for society at large, since it opens the possibility of challenging the ideology of success and recognition on which the perpetuation of neoliberalism relies.

At the end of her study on the impostor, Deutsch pessimistically concluded that the more research she did, the more she started seeing impostors everywhere: among her friends and acquaintances, even herself. Everyone seems to fabricate their identity in accordance with some imaginary concept of self. Deutsch questioned whether there is a difference between the "normal" and the pathological impostor and whether a direct identification of ego ideal with the self is actually only achieved by saints, geniuses, and psychotics: "As one's ego ideal can never be completely gratified from *within*, we direct our demands to the external world, *pretending . . . that we actually are what we would like to be*."[15] While Deutsch is right to see elements of imposture in everyone, the problem is not that people pretend that they are whom they would like to be, but that they are constantly guessing whom they would like to be and which of their images might be socially desirable. As a result, as painters in the past often experimented with different styles of self-portrait, nowadays people take selfie after selfie—constantly in search of the perfect image and never finding it. And when people share these images with others, they are over and over again dealing with the question of whether they are being acknowledged or ignored.

7

The Delusion of
Big Data

TODAY, PEOPLE ARE NOT ONLY being monitored by others, they are increasingly monitoring themselves. Although we generally "agree" to allow access to our data when we use self-monitoring apps, we tend to ignore the fact that such software invites corporations and state surveillance systems to use our data in ways that may be against our own best interest. The accumulation of "big data" has resulted in a profusion of new knowledge about who we are and what we do, individually and collectively. Concurrently, new forms of ignorance and denial have emerged as defenses and reactions to this "wealth" of new information.

The Passion for Self-Surveillance

The market is flooded with devices that are designed to help us navigate our daily lives so that we will become more productive, better organized, healthier, slimmer, and less stressed. Many of the applications installed on smartphones claim to speed up achievement of these goals through measurement. People can thus measure their calories, the steps they take, how far they run, their menstrual cycles, and—during pregnancy—even the heartbeat of their unborn child.

It is hard to find anything in previous generations that is comparable to this new culture of counting steps, heartbeats, or calories. Sociologists researching postindustrial capitalism and its insistence on increased productivity link the obsession with measurement to new forms of social control and the monitoring of factory workers' every move.[1] Keeping track of productivity in the workplace has now extended to people's private lives and their homes. The goals of personal achievement, success, and happiness that drive postindustrial capitalism have given birth to the wellness industry and a vast array of self-help enterprises.[2] This flourishing market has become the prime promoter of the notion that proper measurement, tracking, and self-control are essential to attaining these goals.

This obsession, however, is deeply problematic for three reasons. First, people generally find it hard to follow self-improvement programs for a long time; second, partly because of their failure to stick to these programs long term, they can experience increased anxiety or feelings of guilt; and third, the new technologies that monitor activity allow for the collection of personal data that is subject to uses and abuses that are hard to imagine and harder to control.

Personal measurement and tracking are promoted as strategies that can make self-transformation manageable and predictable. The numbers that are recorded on monitoring devices are also supposed to encourage a sense of achievement and thus build resistance to the temptation to revert to less healthy ways of being; they operate as self-binding mechanisms.

Many centuries ago, Homer recognized the need for self-binding when he had Odysseus tie himself to his ship's mast to avoid succumbing to the Sirens' song. Jon Elster also links the idea of self-binding to various strategies people use when they wish to change a particular behavior.[3] For example, someone who wants to stop smoking may announce this intention to colleagues and friends and, by doing so, be less inclined—because of guilt or embarrassment—to light a cigarette in their presence.

The internet allows for self-binding strategies that also rely on social pressure, even though there is no face-to-face contact with people online. Dieters who log their daily food intake on an online forum, for instance, may feel ashamed to have to admit their failure to follow their diet plan to strangers online.

If online communication with anonymous interlocutors can motivate people to change their behavior, what happens when they try to change their habits with the help of private self-monitoring devices?

The Failure of Self-Monitoring

Although people may fervently download self-help apps, many soon forget about them and, for one reason or another, stop measuring their progress.[4] Researchers who were trying to understand why apps are so soon forgotten and lifestyle gurus trying to encourage better habits rediscovered Aristotle's term "akrasia," which describes the way we can sometimes act against our own better judgment. Today the term is most commonly used for a form of procrastination that stops people from following through with their plans even when they know it is in their own best interest to do so.[5]

A number of interesting studies about akrasia and tracking devices have been carried out in the field of medicine. In one study, people who were asked to monitor their physical activity got paid for increasing the total number of steps they walked per day.[6] During the study, when the subjects were financially compensated for being more physically active, it looked as if they were easily able to change their lifestyle and improve their health. The expectation was that increased well-being would help them continue with the plan when money ceased to be the motivating factor. But for the majority of participants, this was not the case. When the financial benefit ended, so did most of the physical activity.

Whether money should be used as an incentive to change habits is open to debate.[7] But for the purposes of the argument here, it may be more useful to look at the failure of self-monitoring through the lens of psychology. In the last two decades, psychological studies of willpower have relied heavily on a study that tested willpower through two related exercises.[8] Roy Baumeister and his colleagues first examined willpower by telling two groups of people what to eat. Both groups had chocolate cookies and a bowl of radishes in front of them. One group was asked to eat only the radishes, while the other group was allowed to eat both the radishes and the cookies. The idea was to measure how much self-discipline it would take for the radish-restricted group to resist the cookies.

After this first exercise, both groups were then asked to solve puzzles that were designed to be unsolvable. It turned out that the group allowed to eat cookies spent much longer trying to solve the puzzles than the radish eaters. One explanation put forward was that willpower is like a muscle that can be strengthened with regular exercise, but if it is used too much, its strength is depleted. So if the radish eaters exhausted all their willpower trying not to eat the cookies, they would have none left to force themselves to solve the puzzle. In contrast, the cookie eaters, who did not need to exercise their willpower in the first experiment, were able to apply it in the second experiment, in which they stupidly persisted in efforts to solve puzzles that their non-cookie-eating colleagues (with presumably sugar-free brains) recognized as unsolvable and left unsolved.

In the last few years, the failure to replicate Baumeister's experiment has led psychologists to conclude that "willpower *isn't* a limited resource, but believing that it is makes you less likely to follow through on your plans."[9] According to this newer perspective, a self-fulfilling prophecy is at work: if we presuppose that restraining ourselves will exhaust our willpower and thereby cause us to fail in our efforts to follow through on other projects, then that failure is likely to occur when we are put to the test. However, if we do not presuppose that something called "willpower fatigue" exists, that failure is less likely to happen.

Other studies have tried to assess how emotions might influence our ability to follow the plans we have made to change our behavior. Some self-help books advise that we try to be aware of the emotions we feel when following, say, a new health regimen and, rather than use all our energy dealing with negative emotions, try to redirect that energy toward creating an environment for ourselves that supports our goals.[10]

Which is where apps and wearable technology come in. They are supposed to help us create just such a positive environment so that we can more easily follow through with our personal improvement plans. The idea is that if we set clear goals for changing our lives, the apps will then help us realize them. Unfortunately, the reality is that people who download apps and buy wearable devices can just as easily "forget" to track whatever they planned to track and start ignoring their set goals as those who don't use the devices, so there has now emerged a new kind of device specifically designed to increase our feelings of guilt or anxiety about not using the old devices.

For example, a wristband device called Pavlok offers people a way to punish themselves when they do not follow through with their plans by enabling the wearer to zap him- or herself with a light electric shock if tempted to do something that he or she shouldn't. With this shock, Pavlok is supposed to arouse the inner voice that says, "Wake up, sleepy head, it's time to go to the gym!"; "Put down those chips!"; or "Stop wasting time on Facebook!" The makers of Pavlok claim that the device helps unlock people's "true" potential by making them accountable for their behavior and thus better able to change it when necessary. It relies on conditioning exercises in the famous experiment that Ivan Pavlov performed on dogs early in the twentieth century. Just as Pavlov conditioned his dogs to start salivating even when no food was present, the makers of Pavlok claim their device can condition people not to engage in self-damaging behavior. Pavlok wearers have testified that they were able to change their bad habits of overeating, nail biting, hair pulling, or oversleeping because they started associating their bad habits with the prospect of being zapped.[11]

The popularity and proliferation of such devices raise some interesting questions about why people need to measure so many things in life and what they really gain from it. For example, Kérastase, a producer of hair care products, created a new "smart" hairbrush, codesigned with the tech company Withings, that is supposed to assess how people treat their hair. With the help of a built-in microphone, the brush listens as people style their hair and then measures how frizzy or dry their hair is and whether they have split ends.[12] Another device for runners, the Apple Watch Nike+, comes in two sizes and features built-in GPS tracking, a perforated sports band for ventilation, Nike+ Run Club app integration, and exclusive Siri commands to start a run. Equipped with push notifications, the

Nike+ Run Club app entices wearers to run by offering daily motivations through smart run reminders. For example, "Are we running today?" appears on the watch at the time when the person usually goes for a run. The app also sends and receives challenges between friends and alerts runners about the weather. Not only is training data, including pace, distance, and heart rate, available at a glance, run summaries are also shared with friends to encourage friendly competition.

Constant nudging, comparison with others, and self-punishment are all tactics that the new technologies are harnessing to help people achieve their goals for self-improvement. While some may find this approach helpful, it is worth remembering that the whole ideology of self-improvement can also contribute to feelings of inadequacy, anxiety, and guilt.

As a result, some people may choose to deal with these unpleasant feelings by treating the device not as a guilt-inflicting surrogate superego but rather as a substitute for the self-improving behavior itself. Austrian philosopher Robert Pfaller coined the term "interpassivity" to describe the strategy of using a device as an intermediary that performs certain acts instead of the person.[13] An example is a person who frequently records movies but never watches them. By recording the films, the person is able to do other things while feeling that the recorder in a sense "watches" the movie instead.[14] The same is true of a meditation app. I download it, pay for it, and perform some meditations that it guides me to do, but within a few days I learn to ignore it. Since I have it on my device, the app can be taken as a stand-in for my meditation practice, so that it is "doing" meditation for me, interpassively, while I go on performing my other, possibly more enjoyable, daily tasks. Using an app in such an interpassive way might allow people to ignore the feeling of anxiety and guilt that they might have otherwise experienced by failing to fulfill their goals.

The proliferation of these apps and wearable devices is based on the idea that people can be successfully manipulated into performing in a way that is more productive and less self-damaging. When they are promoted by employers, one may assume that the goal is to create workers who are healthier, more motivated, and more focused, which causes them to perform better in the workplace, be more productive, and cost less. When people ignore apps and wearable devices that are supposed to make their lives more productive, it is not that they are consciously embracing self-destructive behavior. Rather, they are being driven by something that cannot be controlled or easily altered—their unconscious desires, fantasies, and drives. The fact that people so quickly give up on their goals, forget about self-improvement apps, or use them in an interpassive way should not be taken as a sign that they are not trying to make changes in their lives, but rather as proof that these changes do not come easily, however rational people's goals, because a person's unconscious often acts against his or her own well-being.

If people easily forget the various apps they have downloaded to change their behavior and for some the very fact of downloading an app seems enough to make them feel better, the problem is that the apps do not forget the people who have downloaded them.

Disregard and Denial about Big Data

While most of the discussions about wearable technologies focus on whether they really can change people's behavior and why people so quickly start ignoring them, another form of disregard—about the data that these devices collect—is rarely talked about, even though it is common knowledge that companies that sell apps and wearable technology collect and sell the data of their users.

Amy Pittman recalls a time when she was trying to get pregnant and became enthusiastic about a period tracker:

> Like many 20-somethings, I have an app for just about every important thing in my life. I have a health tracker that I ignore, a budget tracker that I ignore, an app to pay my bills that I try to ignore, and a period tracker that I'm obsessed with. Every week, I religiously tracked my mood on the period tracker along with my core temperature, the viscosity of various fluids, how often my husband and I were having sex, if sperm was present, etc. The app had more intimate knowledge of my reproductive behavior than my husband or any doctor. On the day of my positive pregnancy test, I logged into my period tracker to share the good news. When I did, it suggested a pregnancy app, which I downloaded immediately. It was full of bright colors and interactive graphics.[15]

But then Pittman miscarried. She immediately deactivated her pregnancy-monitoring app. But logging off from the app did not prevent various marketing companies from continuing to send her info on pregnancy and baby products. The maker of her pregnancy app had sold her data to marketing companies; however, when Pittman logged a miscarriage into the app and stopped using it, that information was not passed along. Pittman describes a shocking event: "Seven months after my miscarriage, mere weeks before my due date, I came home from work to find a package on my welcome mat. It was a box of baby formula bearing the note: 'We may all do it differently, but the joy of parenthood is something we all share.'"[16]

A whole new surveillance domain has opened up with the help of big data that allows commercial companies, as well as the state, to monitor people's daily lives. At the start of this period of massive data collection, it is almost certain that most people did not understand the market that existed for data collected about them. Now that various media routinely address the problem of surveillance, however, it is not so much a lack of knowledge that is at work in the way people deal with their personal data, but rather a denial of that knowledge.

With regard to the various kinds of information that is being collected, we can observe strategies of denial similar to those used when people are informed that they are seriously ill. People who have witnessed or read about cases of personal data being mishandled do not think that something like that might happen to them. Some may not even be bothered that their data is being passed on to corporations or the state. Still others may be very sensitive to anyone listening in on their phone conversations, but they are not concerned that data about their bodies is being recorded by a fitness or pregnancy tracker. Similar problems apply to genetic information collected by commercial DNA testing companies, which can easily be handed to the government or sold to other commercial companies without the user clearly understanding how his or her data can be misappropriated and monetized.[17]

If we apply Nancy Tuana's taxonomy of ignorance, which was mentioned in chapter 1, we can observe all four ways of "not knowing" at work in the way people engage with big data.[18] We might not know what the data collected about us is used for and might not care about it. We might not know that we do not know what happens with the data. It is possible that companies that collect the data do not want us to know. And it is also possible that we resort to willful ignorance—that is, denial—since in this case we know that data is collected, that it is sold, and that it can be abused, but we simply resolve not to care about it. And sometimes our willed ignorance is informed by the belief, "I have nothing to hide."

Another explanation of ignorance with regard to big data is
that data is collected by potentially powerful interests for purposes that are not fully understood.[19] Here, ignorance pertains
not so much to how data is collected but rather to how it is used.
The business of corporations who traffic in data, the mechanisms of data mining, and the working of algorithms remain so
alien and opaque that most people cannot envision what such
data can be used for or how it can be manipulated. Keeping data
opaque and algorithms a secret contributes to strategic ignorance, where those in power profit by keeping the majority in
the dark.[20]

Informed Consent

Whenever we download apps, sign up for free internet access
in public spaces, register for loyalty cards, or put on wearable
technology, we are usually asked to tick a box giving our consent to data collection. Our reaction to consent forms with
regard to big data involves strategies of ignorance similar to
those we observe in medicine. Most often, we give our consent
without reading the long document that, in very small print
and bureaucratic and legalistic language, informs us of the
rights of the service provider. We automatically click the box
on the consent form and hope to start using the service without further interruptions. If we were to read all the various informed consent documents that we usually blindly approve, it
is quite possible that we would not install some apps on our
phones, put on wearable technology, or connect to open internet servers.

But if we so easily ignore what we have given our consent
to, one must question the purpose of engaging a customer in
this game of consent. The problem with informed consent is

that it primarily protects the provider of a service, while for the consumer it more and more presents a case of a forced choice. We are offered a choice either to consent to give away our data or to refuse to give it away. However, if we say no, we lose the possibility of enjoying the device or service that collects the data. Similarly, if we do not consent to allow ourselves to be monitored by internet providers, we are denied access to the internet in the first place. In cases of forced choice, one is in principle offered a choice; however, this choice involves only one option. In a way, choice is offered and denied at the same time.

An example of forced choice existed in socialist Yugoslavia when young men were obliged to serve in the army. When young men became conscripts, they had to go through a ritual where they took an oath saying that they freely chose to become a member of the Yugoslav army. However, one man took this choice seriously and said that since becoming a member of the army was a matter of choice, he chose not to join it. When this happened, he was immediately sent to prison. The choice in question was offered and denied at the same time.

Jacques Lacan explained the idea of forced choice by envisioning a situation where a man is confronted by a robber who demands, "Your money or your life!" This demand puts the man in a position of forced choice. If he chooses his money, he will lose his life and thus will not be able to enjoy the wealth that he saved. The only choice that is left to him is his life, which, however, will be less enjoyable since he will not have the money.[21]

Similarly, when we are asked to consent to the use of devices that track our data, we are offered a choice: enjoy the app but give consent to use your data, or you can have your life without the app.

Machines Cannot Be Wrong

If some people blindly consent to giving their data away, many others also place their trust in the machines that handle such data. Our belief in the power of computers nowadays is so strong that we often do not even imagine that serious mistakes can be made in the way they are used.

In the early 2000s I presided over a panel that evaluated the output of Slovenian research groups. I was not linked to these research groups, and the evaluators were from abroad. This setting was supposed to allow for an objective assessment of the researchers' work, which, of course, had serious implications for their future funding. My job was fairly simple. On top of facilitating the evaluators' reports, I had to put their marks into an Excel spreadsheet, which in the end would automatically calculate the results, providing me with a list of groups that would get future funding and those that would not. I meticulously recorded the marks on the spreadsheet so that errors would not affect the results, and the software then calculated the cumulative marks and the evaluation was done. A few hours later, I looked at the form again and had the feeling that something was amiss. Groups that consistently got good marks from the evaluators were not as high on the list of results as I had expected. I rechecked whether I had put all the marks onto the form correctly, and it all looked fine. I clicked the calculation button again and got the same results as before. Frustrated, I decided to do the calculation by hand. To my surprise, the results were different. I resisted the possibility that the computer could be wrong and did the calculations again. Finally, I had to conclude that the spreadsheet had not been coded properly. When I contacted the agency that had set it up, at first no one believed me that the machine had produced the wrong results.

Finally, their IT personnel confirmed that there was an error in the algorithm that, as a result of my complaint, they had been able to solve. Until I had that experience, I was a very trusting user of similar forms and spreadsheets. Subsequently, I started wondering how many similar calculation errors are undermining the accuracy of our computer-dependent work and why we do not pay more attention to finding them.

In the world of big data, we have to deal not only with the potential for software failures (bearing in mind that software is only as good as the programmers who write it, as the preceding example shows) but also a high level of opacity related to how data is collected and interpreted, who has access to it, and how it can be manipulated. It is not surprising that such opacity creates new types of ignorance, as well as new fantasies about the information big data provides. When we collect a huge amount of data, people suddenly start seeing patterns in random data where none actually exist, simply because enormous quantities of data can appear to offer connections that radiate in all directions.[22] Researchers of big data call this apophenia.

One of the ways we deal with blind spots is by trying to visualize them. "Gaps" in our knowledge are linked in a very particular way to the fantasies we create around them. An interesting way to explore these fantasies is through art. Many contemporary artists have become fascinated with the new developments in science and use brain images, genetic code, and newly acquired knowledge in the fields of astrophysics and physics in their art. Not surprisingly, big data has also attracted their attention. The Norwegian artist Toril Johannessen, for example, in her art project "Words and Years," uses big data to create pictures that try to alert viewers to important themes in today's world. Combing through data in scientific journals, she created a picture that shows when and with what frequency the word "crisis" is used with regard to nature or society, how often the word "miracle" is used with regard to nature and society, and how many articles in the field of genetics deal with the words "greed" and "desire."[23] Johannessen picked words that are often charged with meaning. In her artwork she visualized them by showing patterns related to the number of times these words are mentioned in scientific journals. While the viewers do not know the context in which the words are used, they are left to imagine what contributes to the increase or decrease of these words in scientific texts. With her artistic take on big data, Johannessen does not offer an understanding of the statistics she plays with but rather exposes the gaps in our understanding of the datafication of life.

Even before the rapid development of data analysis, artists collected data and used them in artwork. In the 1980s, the Russian artists Vitaliy Komar and Alex Melamid conducted surveys in different countries in which they asked people what constitutes a beautiful painting and an ugly one. Universally, the result of the surveys indicated that people perceived a beautiful painting to be one that showed scenes of nature with mountains, a sunny sky, and an animal in the setting, while an ugly painting was perceived to be one that consisted of abstract triangles in dark, unappealing colors. The artists then tried to produce an ideally beautiful painting and an ugly one using the mean results of their survey.[24] Looking at the beautiful and ugly paintings that they then painted incited in the viewer an uncanny feeling—trying to comply with people's idea of what a beautiful or ugly painting looks like took away the edge of surprise that often accompanies good art. By taking seriously what people perceived as beautiful and ugly art, the artists tried to put into words and realize in an image what usually cannot be grasped in a rational way. What makes an artwork great usually escapes words, which is why it is not easy to rationally describe what makes one work beautiful and another ugly.

In order to depict the nature of what cannot easily be put into words or images and what escapes people's conscious perceptions of themselves, as well as the world around them, Lacan used the term "the real." This term does not pertain to what we usually understand as reality, but rather to what escapes the conception of the reality that we form with the help of language and images.

Today we try to come close to this "real" with the help of science and new technology. Genetics and neuroscience allow us to imagine that decoding the genome and perfecting brain scans can help us comprehend what makes us human. We turn to big data in a similar quest to decipher the enigma of subjectivity.

Ignorance and Belief in Progress

We often glorify the pursuit of knowledge; however, the desire to not know is equally important for our survival. Closing our eyes, not seeing something, and not remembering what has been painful or hard to deal with are strategies that people have embraced with a passion equal to the passion with which they have embraced the pursuit of knowledge.

In our lives, repressing something psychologically helps us push away what is consciously hard to accept or comprehend. But with ignorance, it is as if we have all the information needed to comprehend something but it does not relate to us. An individual, for example, can have information about a threat but behave as if the threat does not apply to or concern him or her. This kind of ignorance paradoxically contributes to a feeling of omnipotence; we perceive ourselves as being more powerful than we actually are, almost invincible.

If we compare ignorance of the use of big data with climate change denial, we can see a similarity in the way these two forms of closing our eyes to difficult things link to our ideas of progress. Until the widespread protests related to climate change started in 2019, people in the developed world were often afraid to admit that the progress or development that underlies modern capitalism cannot last forever. People were also afraid to face the prospect that climate change might cause a decline in economic growth. Equally troubling for some were government interventions in the market through various mechanisms to control carbon dioxide emissions, along with penalties for corporations. Such interventions implied a loss of freedom, which for many people is inherent to the operation of the free market. Even those who were aware of the warnings that scientists were and are issuing about climate change often adopted various strategies that enabled them to believe that these warnings did not affect them personally.

People often deny that the reality of climate change means that they personally need to change their behavior and that society needs to change its approach to continued growth and development. This denial is related to the fact that people are afraid of change and they are anxious about what potential changes might mean for their own future, without thinking about the impact of their refusal to act on future generations. They want to hold on to an idea of continued progress, the price for which will have to be paid by the next generation. The incredibly rapid development of the past is simply not sustainable, based as it is on energy that we obtain from fossil fuels.[25] The prosperity that people in the developed world have enjoyed as the result of an economy based on fossil fuels has allowed them to live longer, healthier lives, but this prosperity has been founded on an increasingly willed ignorance of the impact of that economy on the world as a whole.

For a long time, we have also had an overoptimistic idea of how big data contributes to progress. In addition to problems involving the mismanagement of data, and new forms of surveillance, future generations will need to deal with the fact that they never consented to any of their data being collected. Current notions of privacy and informed consent do not take into account that data on infants and children is now being collected on a massive scale without their consent and without them being able to control or comprehend the impact that this data collection will have on their future lives.[26]

Optimistic big data researchers like to point out that big data should not be regarded from a negative perspective alone. People can be empowered to use data to their advantage, and data that is available through open access can significantly contribute to scientific research and social change.

Proponents of big data thus like to point out that individuals should have access to their data so that they can make full use of it. The idea is that people's tracking devices and computers know more about their habits than individuals consciously do. Knowing about the data that is collected about oneself will help one navigate a better life. Mark Andrejevic, an academic and expert on critical data studies, warns against such enthusiasm by pointing out that there exists a great discrepancy in power between those who collect big data and those who are the objects of such collection: "Even if users had access to their own data, they would not have the pattern recognition or predictive capabilities of those who can mine aggregated databases. Moreover, even if individuals were provided with everyone else's data (a purely hypothetical conditional), they would lack the storage capacity and processing power to make sense of the data and put it to use."[27] Furthermore, having the right information or the right amount of it may not be enough to motivate change for the better.

At the start of 2020, when Coronavirus disease 2019 (COVID-19) was spreading rapidly in China, there was insufficient information about the virus to alert Western governments to the urgency of implementing early strategies for containment. Not enough modeling had been done of its possible spread, so that at the start of the pandemic in Europe there was genuine ignorance about what people were dealing with. But even when data did start to become available, state leaders in countries like the United States and the United Kingdom ignored it for several crucial weeks, deciding to hide their heads in the sand for a mixture of political and economic reasons. It was only when the scientific community strongly condemned their willful ignorance and inaction and the death toll in their own countries started to rise that these leaders began to implement the emergency measures that had already been implemented elsewhere several weeks earlier. With these measures also came new ways of collecting data from the general public without them knowing about it or being asked for their consent.

The doctors who first alerted the public that they were dealing with a highly contagious virus were also ignored in China and the first whistleblowers were silenced. But when the virus started spreading and the Chinese authorities realized the seriousness of the situation, they quickly imposed a strict quarantine, which was implemented with the help of mass surveillance that relied on mass collection of data from mobile phone companies tracking people's movements, as well as cameras in public places and increased use of facial recognition technology. In Iran, when the virus started spreading in February 2020, people were advised to download an app that claimed to give information about the symptoms of the coronavirus infection.[28] This app, however, was designed to track people's movements and provide that information to the government. In South Korea, people's movements were tracked using GPS phone data, credit card records, and interviews with each infected person about his or her movements.[29]

In March 2020, the Israeli government imposed emergency measures that allowed its internal security agency, Shin Bet, to have access to location data of the mobile phones of people infected with the virus for the period of two weeks before their infection was established.[30] Such cyber monitoring was justified by the idea that other people who had been in the vicinity of the infected person could be notified and quarantine orders would be more easily enforceable. Legal questions over how data would be collected and stored, what technological means would be employed, whether the data would be used for enforcement purposes only, and when the data would be erased were pushed aside, which increased anxiety over the collection of data for purposes not related to halting the spread of the virus.[31]

The ignorance many countries first showed with regard to the spread of the coronavirus paradoxically allowed for the implementation of strategies of mass surveillance and data collection when these governments later changed course. It was as if the ignorance that they first resorted to increased the levels of anxiety in the general public, which in turn made the public less concerned about the collection of data from their mobile phones. The worry is that when governments claim the right to track individuals or groups of people in a time of crisis, when the crisis is over they rarely return to prior norms. Given that people willfully expose themselves and share details of their private lives freely online in normal times, in the extraordinary times there may be even more willingness to allow governments to violate their privacy in the sincere hope of stopping the spread of the virus.[32] In the long run, however, people's ignorance, as well as their powerlessness over what happens with their data, who has access to it, and whether they will continue to be tracked when the crisis is over, may come at the cost of increased surveillance and even greater disregard for people's rights.

Conclusion

IN THE EARLY TWENTIETH CENTURY, American anthropologist Paul Radin studied the Winnebago tribe of Native Americans (now known as the Ho-Chunk Nation), which consisted of two kinship groups living in the same village. Radin was surprised to observe that when these two groups were asked to describe the structure of the village, they did so in very different ways. When he asked the first group to draw their settlement, they presented a village plan showing houses positioned in a circle where the houses of the members of the two groups were clustered together, whereas the second group drew a very different image: there was an imaginary divide across the layout of the village, with the houses of one group positioned on one side of the divide, and the houses of the other group on the other side.[1]

When anthropologist Claude Lévi-Strauss analyzed these drawings, he reasoned that the key question was not what the actual plan of the village was, but instead why the two groups perceived the reality so differently. He said that the difference in perception needed to be understood in the context of the complex relationships that existed between the two groups. Members of the groups tried to conceptualize this complexity according to their position in the social structure. Even more importantly, depending on their particular perception of what their village looked like, each group was able to regard itself and the other group as either central or peripheral, and to retain their status.[2]

Today, it seems that we are living in a world that is observed radically differently by people who live in the same place. In the United States, Republicans and Democrats see their own country, as well as the world, in opposing ways. In the United Kingdom, supporters of Brexit and its opponents present images of their country as if they live poles apart. In Australia, at the time of the massive bush fires at the start of 2020, it was as if the government, together with other, corporate climate change deniers, did not see the reality of the destruction that was happening in their own country.

Coronavirus disease 2019 (COVID-19) has been one of the most significant unknowns of the start of the twenty-first century. The fact that the virus is invisible and new and that no cure or vaccination existed when it started spreading globally helped lead countries to start drawing the world map very differently when it came to acknowledging its existence. Just as the Winnebago moieties perceived their village in the way that allowed them to keep their status, for a long time the countries without coronavirus cases saw the infection as something that ravaged countries elsewhere, far away, and that they were somehow magically protected from.

In December 2019, the Chinese authorities ignored doctors who warned that a new type of pneumonia was emerging among their patients. It was only at the start of January 2020 that the authorities admitted the rapid spread of the infection. Soon massive lockdowns were imposed first in Wuhan and later in other Chinese cities. When tens of thousands of people had become infected and hundreds had died in China and the infection was already spreading in many Asian countries, the United States and the majority of countries in Europe behaved as if there were no real danger to their population—as if they were not sharing the same planet. The infection appeared to be happening so far away that people in these places could easily close their eyes to it and push aside the fact that we are living in a globalized world where massive numbers of goods and people are circulating nonstop.

Negation, denial, and ignorance became rampant in the way numerous state leaders responded to COVID-19. Although North Korea borders China, in early March 2020 the leadership reported that they did not have a single case of COVID-19 in the country.[3] When the infection was already spreading rapidly in Russia, Anastasia Vasilyeva, the head of Russia's Alliance of Doctors trade union, warned that officials were classifying coronavirus deaths as pneumonia deaths.[4] By pretending that they were dealing with ordinary pneumonia, the Russian authorities were also able to push aside the fact that their doctors lacked protective gear to treat patients. Doctors' warnings about the lack of masks and other equipment were dismissed as fake news.

At the same time, the Turkish government was still insisting that there were no cases of COVID-19. When President Recep Tayyip Erdoğan finally admitted some infections in his country, the Turkish state-owned press reported, "Turkish genes rendered most Turkish people immune."[5] While the president still encouraged Turks to live their lives normally, the online media started spreading the advice that people could gain protection from the new virus by eating sheep soup, which is why restaurants were barely able to keep up with the demand for this dish.

At a time when the infection was causing devastation in Italy, Spain, and the United States and thousands of people were dying in these countries and elsewhere, Brazilian president Jair Bolsonaro said that COVID-19 was "a symptom-free nuisance for '90 percent' of infected Brazilians."[6] At the same time, Mexican president Andrés Manuel López Obrador was publicly expressing his disbelief in the spread of the new virus and encouraged Mexicans to continue eating in restaurants. And UK prime minister Boris Johnson was boasting that he was still shaking hands not long before he tested positive for COVID-19 in late March 2020.

The growing amount of information that was available about the spread of infection around the world did not stop this ignorance and denial. In some cases ignorance was "strategic," since not noticing what was happening allowed the economy to go on, at least for some time.[7] Coupled with this ignorance was a refusal to acknowledge the importance of many of the people who keep the economy going, as if the health and well-being of low-paid, ordinary workers is not a prerequisite for the economy to function. In addition, there was denial related to the belief that the new virus killed mostly old and infirm people, not the young and productive, which opened the door to ageism and ableism.[8] The transmission of fake news through social media amplified people's confusion about what was happening with the pandemic. From the start, conspiracy theories multiplied and countries blamed each other. While some conspiracy theories embraced the idea that the virus originated in the Chinese center for bioweapons, others claimed that it was the United States that manufactured it. The media were also full of false claims about what might cure the virus, what might make it worse, what measures authorities were suggesting to curb infections, and what technologies were contributing to its spread.[9]

Before the pandemic started, Danish and American political scientists Michael Bang Petersen, Mathias Osmundsen, and

Kevin Arceneaux questioned the motives of people who use the internet to spread fake news, conspiracy theories, or politically motivated attacks. Interviews with these people revealed that they did not believe the stories they were sharing were true. What mattered to them was provoking anger, with some respondents saying they enjoyed the chaos they created. Some people admitted that they fantasized about a natural disaster wiping out most of humanity so that a small group of people could start again from scratch. And 24 percent of the more than six thousand people surveyed believed society "should be burned to the ground." The researchers reasoned that this need for chaos is, for some, linked to the loss of status, the feeling of having been left out in our highly unequal society.[10]

This research shows that the problem is not that people who feel ignored have a greater tendency to ignore what is accurate information and what is not. It also does not seem to be the case that these people have a stronger tendency to close their eyes to uncomfortable knowledge. Consciously, they might know very well what is fake news and what not; however, they make psychological gains when they spread false information or conspiracy theories. When Freud talked about the power of the death drive, his point was that it is not simply linked to the will for destruction, but also to the desire to start anew, to create from zero or, as Jacques Lacan said, to create ex nihilo.[11] If one were to question what this renewed world would look like, usually the people who fantasize about destruction do not envision themselves gone. But as with HIV, which I talked about in chapter 4, there were also people who found enjoyment in exposing themselves to the virus.[12] While world leaders like Donald Trump, Bolsonaro, and Johnson warned the public that they would lose loved ones, they were in denial that they themselves might succumb to the new illness.

The COVID-19 pandemic opened up the possibility of global structural change—a radical rethinking of the way today's capitalism has increased inequality and contributed to climate change and how the hunger for profit (which has increasingly ended up in the pockets of the few) has decimated the public sector, impoverished state health care systems, and pushed aside ideas of universal income and a more sustainable economy. Yet world leaders ignored what was happening around them and the actions needed to create a more equal, environmentally friendly society for the future. At the G20 meeting, which, for the first time, happened online in late March 2020, the world leaders embraced denial so that they could continue business as usual.[13] They boasted that the world "will overcome" the pandemic, as if proclamations alone were enough.

As this book has shown, in times of crisis, people individually often embrace ignorance in order to avoid facing up to traumatic events or feelings. For some, however, this ignorance does not involve not knowing; rather, it requires surrender to an endless stream of information. As the coronavirus pandemic was rampaging around the world, a friend of mine became a connoisseur of the news. He appeared to be the most informed person I knew about what the science was saying, what protective measures doctors were advising people to take, and what was happening with the infection around the world. Then one day he admitted to me that reading all this news was not a search for understanding but rather a desperate attempt to find proof that the pandemic was not real.

ACKNOWLEDGMENTS

I thank John Stubbs, Jane Malmo, and Susan Tucker for their immense help in correcting my English and for giving me many valuable suggestions on the theme of this book. Sarah Caro has been an editor an author can only dream about. She has given me numerous ideas on how to better present my arguments. I am grateful to Sarah Chalfant and Emma Smith from the Wylie Agency for their encouragement and support, and to the whole team at Princeton University Press for their hard work.

Darian Leader, Devorah Baum, and Josh Appignanesi have read the entire manuscript, and I am grateful for their most helpful comments. Discussions with Henrietta Moore, Brigitte Balbure, Genevieve Morel, Mateja Bučar, and Maja Hawlina have allowed me to look at ignorance from unexpected angles. My son Tim and my partner Branko have been the best conversation partners one can have, while daily chats with my sister Tanja and my mother Hilda have provided much-needed respite from writing. My late father Hubert provided valuable memories of ignorance after World War II that I reflect upon in chapter 2.

I am thankful to my colleagues at the Institute of Criminology at the Faculty of Law in Ljubljana, Slovenia, for creating such a welcome, engaging, and warm working environment, and to my colleagues and students from the School of Law, Birkbeck College, University of London, for many stimulating discussions.

Parts of chapter 2 have been published in the *Journal of the Centre for Freudian Analysis and Research,* no. 27 (2016). Some of the ideas presented in chapter 3 have previously appeared in *Diacritics* 47, no. 1 (2019). An earlier version of the argument developed in chapter 7 has been published in the collection of essays *Big Data, Crime, and Social Control,* edited by Aleš Završnik (London: Routledge, 2019).

I acknowledge financial support from the Slovenian Research Agency (research core funding No P5-0221 and research project No J5-8242). I have also received funding from the European Union's Horizon 2020 research and innovation program under the Marie Skłodowska-Curie grant agreement No 734855.

NOTES

Introduction

1. Katie Rogers and Maggie Haberman, "Trump Now Claims He Always Knew the Coronavirus Would Be a Pandemic," *New York Times*, March 17, 2020, https://www.nytimes.com/2020/03/17/us/politics/trump-coronavirus.html.

2. *Merriam-Webster*, s.v. "passion (*n.*)," https://www.merriam-webster.com/dictionary/passion, accessed April 30, 2020.

3. Jamie Holmes, *Nonsense: The Power of Not Knowing* (New York: Crown, 2015).

4. William Davis, *Nervous States: How Feeling Took Over the World* (London: Jonathan Cape, 2018).

5. There is also tactical ignorance, which helps preserve "deniability and innocence, for keeping options open, for avoiding responsibility, but also for assuring fairness and just decisions." Daniel R. DeNicola, *Understanding Ignorance: The Surprising Impact of What We Don't Know* (Cambridge, MA: MIT Press, 2017), 84.

Chapter 1

1. Sam Knight, "Is a High IQ a Burden as Much as a Blessing?," *Financial Times*, April 10, 2009, https://www.ft.com/content/4add9230-23d5-11de-996a-00144feabdco.

2. Richard S. Tedlow, *Denial: Why Business Leaders Fail to Look Facts in the Face—and What to Do about It* (London: Penguin, 2010).

3. Tedlow, *Denial*, xxii.

4. Tedlow, *Denial*, xv.

5. George Orwell, *1984* (London: Penguin, 1956), 169.

6. Orwell, *1984*, 169.

7. Henrik Ibsen, *The Wild Duck* (New York: Dover Thrift Editions, 2000).

8. Studies in social psychology have looked at the so-called Dunning-Kruger effect, which shows that people have problems with assessing their own competence. Often, the less competent that one is, the less capable he or she is of recognizing his

or her incompetence. See Justin Kruger and David Dunning, "Unskilled and Unaware of It: How Difficulties in Recognizing One's Own Incompetence Lead to Inflated Self-Assessments," *Journal of Personality and Social Psychology* 77, no. 6 (1999): 1121–34.

9. Thomas Gilovich, *How We Know What Isn't So: The Fallibility of Human Reason in Everyday Life* (New York: Free Press, 1991), 77.

10. Ann Kerwin, "None Too Solid: Medical Ignorance," *Knowledge* 15, no. 2 (December 1, 1993): 166–85. These concepts of ignorance are further exemplified in Marlys Hearst Witte, Peter Crown, Michael Bernas, and Charles L. Witte, "Lessons Learned from Ignorance: The Curriculum on Medical (and Other) Ignorance," in *The Virtues of Ignorance: Complexity, Sustainability, and the Limits of Knowledge*, ed. Bill Vitek and Wes Jackson (Lexington: University Press of Kentucky, 2010), 253.

11. Nancy Tuana, "The Speculum of Ignorance: The Women's Health Movement and Epistemologies of Ignorance," *Hypatia* 21, no. 3 (August 1, 2006): 1–19.

12. I rely on amended translations of passages from Nicolaus de Cusa, *De Docta Ignorantia*, presented in Fred Dallmayr, *In Search of the Good Life: A Pedagogy for Troubled Times* (Lexington: University Press of Kentucky, 2007), 70. Dallmayr amended translations by Jasper Hopkins presented in Hopkins, *Nicholas of Cusa on Learned Ignorance: A Translation and an Appraisal of "De Docta Ignorantia"* (Minneapolis: Arthur J. Banning, 1981).

13. Dallmayr, *In Search of the Good Life*, 70.

14. Dallmayr, *In Search of the Good Life*, 70.

15. Sigmund Freud, "Negation," in *The Standard Edition of the Complete Psychological Works of Sigmund Freud*, ed. James Strachey et al., vol. 19 (1923–1925), *The Ego and the Id and Other Works* (London: Vintage Classics, 2001), 235–39.

16. Psychoanalysis stresses that denials should not be equated with lies. Denials should also not be "taken as moral failure, but rather as human deficiencies." Wilfried Ver Eecke, *Denial, Negation, and the Forces of the Negative: Freud, Hegel, Spitz, and Sophocles* (Albany: State University of New York Press, 2006), 123.

17. Otto Fenichel, *The Psychoanalytic Theory of Neurosis* (New York: Norton, 1996).

18. Sandor S. Feldman, *Mannerisms of Speech and Gestures in Everyday Life* (New York: International Universities Press, 1959).

19. Daisetz Teitaro Suzuki, *Essays in Zen Buddhism: First Series* (London: Rider, 1958), 129.

20. Suzuki, *Essays in Zen Buddhism*, 128.

21. Milton J. Horowitz, *Stress Response Syndromes* (Oxford: Jason Aronson, 1976).

22. Mark Hobart, "Introduction: The Growth of Ignorance?," in *An Anthropological Critique of Development: The Growth of Ignorance*, ed. Mark Hobart (London: Routledge, 2004), 1–30.

23. Roy Dilley, in his analysis of Senegalese craft practitioners, points out that when craft occupations are perceived as hereditary, the inability to practice a particular skill among the members of a craft-making family opens up complicated questions about knowing and not knowing, as well as the ability to learn. Roy Dilley, "Reflections on Knowledge Practices and the Problem of Ignorance," *Journal of the Royal Anthropological Institute* 16 (2010): S176–92.

24. Ellen Barry, "How to Get Away with Murder in Small-Town India," *New York Times*, August 19, 2017, https://www.nytimes.com/2017/08/19/world/asia/murder-small-town-india.html?action=click&module=RelatedCoverage&pgtype=Article&region=Footer.

25. Suhasini Raj and Ellen Barry, "Indian Police Files Murder Charges after Times Describes Cover-Up," *New York Times*, September 18, 2017, https://www.nytimes.com/2017/09/18/world/asia/india-murder.html?searchResultPosition=1.

26. Charles W. Mills, "Global White Ignorance," in *Routledge International Handbook of Ignorance Studies*, ed. Matthias Gross and Linsey McGoey (London: Routledge, 2015), 217–27.

27. Tod Hartman, "On the Ikeaization of France," *Public Culture* 19, no. 3 (2007): 483–98.

28. Lisa K. Son and Nate Kornell, "The Virtues of Ignorance," *Behavioral Processes* 83, no. 2 (February 2010): 207–12.

29. Stuart Firestein, *Ignorance: How It Drives Science* (Oxford: Oxford University Press, 2012).

30. Joanne Roberts and John Armitage, "The Ignorance Economy," *Prometheus* 26, no. 4 (2008): 346.

31. Robert N. Proctor, "Agnotology: A Missing Term to Describe the Cultural Production of Ignorance (and Its Study)," in *Agnotology: The Making and Unmaking of Ignorance*, ed. Robert N. Proctor and Linda Schiebinger (Stanford, CA: Stanford University Press, 2008), 1–35.

Chapter 2

1. Beth Kampschror, "Alija Goes Bye-Bye: Bosnia's President Retires Gracefully," *Central Europe Review* 2, no. 36 (October 23, 2000), https://www.pecina.cz/files/www.ce-review.org/00/36/kampschror36.html.

2. Why are so many Bosnians in St. Louis? One explanation is that at the time of the Bosnian war, when the refugees started coming to the United States, the State Department closely collaborated with the St. Louis Resettlement Institute and started placing many refugees in this city. Since there were already some Bosnian families in the town, this helped with the resettlement. In addition, a very engaged university librarian arranged for the university to offer many scholarships to young

Bosnian people. When the Bosnian community started growing in St. Louis, its members established many service centers where people spoke in their mother tongue. Because of this development, many Bosnians who were originally placed in other parts of the United States started moving to St. Louis. Now the community is about seventy thousand strong. They have a Bosnian newspaper, there are doctors and lawyers who speak the Bosnian language, and many shops sell produce from the republic of the former Yugoslavia.

3. The International Criminal Tribunal for the Former Yugoslavia indicted Ratko Mladić in 1994 for genocide, crimes against humanity, and numerous war crimes. His trial in The Hague, however, only started in 2012, since he was in hiding until 2011.

4. International Tribunal for the Former Yugoslavia, trial of Radko Mladić, testimony on July 9, 2012, http://www.icty.org/x/cases/mladic/trans/en/120709IT.htm.

5. Ertana's father, Sukrija, is the founder of *Sabah*, the Bosnian newspaper in St. Louis. When he was asked what it is that he remembers from war most vividly, his answer was, "The smell of death, the smell of dead bodies." Doug Moore, "Bosnia: Bosnians in St. Louis Area Mark a Time of Trouble," STLtoday, April 4, 2012, https://www.stltoday.com/news/local/metro/bosnians-in-st-louis-area-mark-a-time-of-trouble/article_689876da-f739-5858-9444-04c2a5367749.html.

6. Moore, "Bosnia."

7. A hidden trauma in the refugee community is a conflict that many older refugees have with their own children. The latter usually learned English properly and are often placed in the position of family translator. They also learned the laws of their new country and sometimes use them to their advantage. If, for example, they have conflict with their parents, they might threaten them by saying that they will report child abuse to the police. Paradoxically, in some cases children become the new persecutors of people who escaped the drama of the war.

8. Todd Dean, "How to Measure What: Universals, Particulars and Subjectivity," in *On Psychoanalysis and Violence: Contemporary Lacanian Perspectives*, ed. Vanessa Sinclair and Manya Steinkoler (London: Routledge, 2018), 127–36.

9. Dean points out that in the former Yugoslavia everyone knows someone who was killed or put into prison for talking freely, which is why talk therapy exposes a lot of anxieties for this generation and is often coupled with the inability to open up.

10. Dori Laub and Nanette C. Auerhahn, "Knowing and Not Knowing Massive Psychic Trauma: Forms of Traumatic Memory," *International Journal of Psychoanalysis* 74, no. 2 (1993): 287–302.

11. Ruth Wajnryb, *The Silence: How Tragedy Shapes Talk* (Crows Nest, New South Wales: Allen and Unwin, 2002), 165.

12. Jacques Lacan, *The Seminar of Jacques Lacan*, bk. 1, *Freud's Papers on Technique*, ed. Jacques-Alain Miller, trans. John Forrester (New York: W. W. Norton, 1991), 191.

13. A Muslim man from the Serb-dominated part of Bosnia before the war strongly believed in brotherhood and unity of the Yugoslav nations. In the days before the war fully erupted, his neighbors warned him that his life was in danger, which is why he decided to find shelter in the woods near his town. When the war started, he continued hiding in the woods and was forced to stay there for two more years until he was captured by the Serbian army and taken into a camp. He survived both the woods and the camp and ended up as a refugee in Denmark. When he was applying for refugee status, he started denying that the war had ever happened. He told stories about his life in the woods without revealing that he was hiding there because of the war. He also denied that he had suffered any pain from his two years in hiding. However, he continually told stories about terrible things that happened to other people, without ever acknowledging that he may have been recounting his own horrific experiences. The man was advised by his family members to seek therapy, but he refused.

14. Gilead Nachmani, "Trauma and Ignorance," *Contemporary Psychoanalysis* 31, no. 3 (July 1, 1995): 423–50.

15. Nachmani, "Trauma and Ignorance," 424.

16. Julio A. Granel, "Considerations on the Capacity to Change, the Clash of Identifications and Having Accidents," *International Review of Psycho-Analysis* 14 (1987): 483–90.

17. Wilfred R. Bion, *Seven Servants* (New York: Jason Aronson, 1977).

18. Amor Mašović and colleagues have helped to identify more than six thousand people killed in Srebrenica.

19. Sonali Deraniyagala, in her book *Wave: A Memoir of Life after Tsunami* (London: Virago, 2013), writes about the loss of her sons, husband, and parents at the time of the 2004 tsunami in Sri Lanka. Here too a piece of clothing plays an important role in the search for the remains of loved ones. When the mother discovers the green T-shirt of her lost son, she loses hope that he might still be alive.

20. Amor Mašovič, "Genocid brez konca," interview by Branko Soban, in *Zločin brez kazni* (Ljubljana: Sanje, 2013), 127–33.

21. Rachel E. Cyr, "Testifying Absence in the Era of Forensic Testimony," *International Journal of Politics, Culture, and Society* 26, no. 1 (2013): 101.

22. Ostoja Marjanović was director of the mining company near Prijedor at the time of the Bosnian war. In 2013, mass graves with hundreds of dead bodies covered by clay were discovered in two of the mines. When, two years later, Marjanović appeared as a witness at the Hague tribunal, he claimed no knowledge of the mass graves and said he had no clue where the bodies might have come from. When he was further asked whether he knew that in 1992 non-Serbs were killed in one of the mines, however, he said that it was possible that happened. Marjanović's claim that he had no knowledge of the crimes that happened at the mines was extraordinary,

since it was well known that the mines were used as a detention center for non-Serbs at the time of the war. Without the forensic discovery of the bodies twenty years after the crimes were committed, it might have been possible that the truth of what happened to the people from these detention centers would not have been revealed. Denis Dzidic, "Bosnia Discovers Two Wartime Mass Graves," *Balkan Transitional Justice*, June 9, 2015, https://balkaninsight.com/2015/06/09/bosnia-discovers-two -wartime-mass-graves/.

23. Cyr, "Testifying Absence in the Era of Forensic Testimony."

24. Lara J. Nettelfield and Sarah E. Wagner, *Srebrenica in the Aftermath of Genocide* (Cambridge: Cambridge University Press, 2014).

25. Jovana Mihajlović Trbovc, "Memory after Ethnic Cleansing: Victims' and Perpetrators' Narratives in Prijedor" [treatises and documents], *Journal of Ethnic Studies* 72 (2014): 25–41.

26. Mihajlović Trbovc, "Memory after Ethnic Cleansing," 28.

27. Mihajlović Trbovc, "Memory after Ethnic Cleansing," 30. When, in June 2013, Bosnian refugees came to Prijedor to commemorate the loss of their family members in the Omarska and other detention camps, they decided to wear white armbands on their sleeves in memory of the armbands that the victims were forced to wear in the camps. One of the local Serbian politicians mocked this commemoration by calling it "yet another gay parade." "Marko Pavić nazvao Dan bijelih traka 'slavljem' i 'gay paradom,'" Klix, June 1, 2013, https://www.klix.ba/vijesti/bih/marko-pavic -nazvao-dan-bijelih-traka-slavljem-i-gay-paradom/130601057.

28. Mihajlović Trbovc, "Memory after Ethnic Cleansing."

29. Colin Freeman, "Ratko Mladic Walks out of Radovan Karadzic War Crimes Trial," *Telegraph*, January 28, 2014, https://www.telegraph.co.uk/news/worldnews /europe/serbia/10601233/Ratko-Mladic-walks-out-of-Radovan-Karadzic-war -crimes-trial.html.

30. Freeman, "Ratko Mladic Walks out of Radovan Karadzic War Crimes Trial."

31. Natalie Huet, "Relief and Justice for Relatives of Srebrenica," *Euronews*, November 22, 2017, https://www.euronews.com/2017/11/22/relief-and-justice-for -relatives-of-srebrenica-victims.

Chapter 3

1. Nikos Panayotopoulos, *Le gène du doute*, trans. Gilles Descorvet (Paris: Gallimard, 2004).

2. Attempts to make such a genetic dating application have provoked criticism because they might open up the door to selective breeding, as well as classify people into "acceptable humans and others." See Courtney Linder, "Harvard Geneticist Wants to Build Dating App That Sure Sounds like Eugenics," *Popular Mechanics*,

December 10, 2019, https://www.popularmechanics.com/science/a30183673/dating
-app-genetics/.

3. Ashifa Kassam, "Sperm Bank Sued as Case of Mentally Ill Donor's History
Unfolds," *Guardian*, April 14, 2016, https://www.theguardian.com/world/2016/apr
/14/sperm-donor-canada-families-file-lawsuit.

4. Greg Land, "Judge Dismisses Third Sperm Bank Lawsuit over Dodgy Donor,"
Law.com, February 26, 2018, https://www.law.com/dailyreportonline/2018/02/26
/judge-dismisses-third-sperm-bank-lawsuit-over-dodgy-donor/?slreturn
=20190901180157.

5. Matthew Renda, "Judge Clears Sperm Bank Fraud Case for Trial," Courthouse
News Service, March 31, 2017, https://www.courthousenews.com/judge-clears
-sperm-bank-fraud-case-trial/.

6. Lindsey Bever, "White Woman Sues Sperm Bank after She Mistakenly Gets
Black Donor's Sperm," *Washington Post*, October 2, 2014, https://www.washington
post.com/news/morning-mix/wp/2014/10/02/white-woman-sues-sperm-bank
-after-she-mistakenly-gets-black-donors-sperm/.

7. Kim Bellware, "White Woman Who Sued Sperm Bank over Black Baby Says
It's Not about Race," Huffington Post, October 2, 2014, https://www.huffingtonpost
.com/2014/10/02/black-sperm-lawsuit_n_5922180.html.

8. Aristotle, *The Metaphysics* (Buffalo, NY: Prometheus Books, 1991).

9. J. Allan Hobson, *Dream Life: An Experimental Memoir* (Cambridge, MA: MIT
Press, 2011).

10. I thank Lizaveta Zeldina for this story.

11. Calvin A. Colarusso, "Living to Die and Dying to Live: Normal and Pathological
Considerations of Death Anxiety," in *The Wound of Mortality: Fear, Denial, and Acceptance of Death*, ed. Salman Akhtar (Lanham, MD: Jason Aronson, 2010), 107–23.

12. Andrée Lehman, "Psychoanalysis and Genetics: Clinical Considerations and
Practical Suggestions," in *Being Human: The Technological Extensions of the Boundaries
of the Body*, ed. Paola Mieli, Jacques Houis, and Mark Stafford (New York: Marsilio,
2000), 201–10.

13. In cases of commercial tests whereby people get information about their potential genetically transmitted illnesses, they often do not get a chance to talk about
their concerns and to get more information about what the risks mean. Carrie Arnold, "'We Are All Mutants Now': The Trouble with Genetic Testing," *Guardian*,
July 18, 2017, https://www.theguardian.com/science/2017/jul/18/we-are-all
-mutants-now-the-trouble-with-genetic-testing.

14. Dirk Lanzerath et al., *Incidental Findings: Scientific, Legal and Ethical Issues*
(Cologne: Deutscher Ärzte-Verlag, 2013).

15. Emiliano Feresin, "Lighter Sentence for Murderer with 'Bad Genes,'" *Nature*,
October 30, 2009.

16. Avshalom Caspi, Joseph McClay, Terrie E. Moffitt, Jonathan Mill, Judy Martin, Ian W. Craig, Alan Taylor, and Richie Poulton, "Role of Genotype in the Cycle of Violence in Maltreated Children," *Science* 297, no. 5582 (August 2, 2002): 851–54.

17. Adrian Raine, *The Anatomy of Violence: The Biological Roots of Crime* (London: Allen Lane, 2013).

18. Dan Malone and Howard Swindle, *America's Condemned: Death Row Inmates in Their Own Words* (Kansas City, MO: Andrews McMeel, 1999), Kindle edition.

19. Raine, *The Anatomy of Violence*, 79.

20. Raine, *The Anatomy of Violence*, 60.

21. In 1995 Landrigan, in his attempt to escape execution, filed a petition for post-conviction relief at Arizona's state court, stating that if his attorney had discussed with him the theory of a biological component of violence in his family, he would have allowed this evidence. While the Arizona state court rejected Landrigan's claim, the US Court of Appeals of the Ninth Circuit in 2006 established that in Landrigan's case there had been ineffective representation of the counsel in allowing him evidentiary hearing.

22. Schriro v. Landrigan, 550 U.S. 465 (2007).

23. Landrigan v. State, 1985 OK CR 52, 700 P.2d 218 (1985).

24. Malone and Swindle, *America's Condemned*, Kindle edition.

25. Evelyn Fox Keller, *The Century of the Gene* (Cambridge, MA: Harvard University Press, 2002).

Chapter 4

1. For more on choice and health, see Renata Salecl, *The Tyranny of Choice* (London: Profile Books, 2010).

2. An example of an immortalist movement is the Eternal Flame Foundation, which later renamed itself People Unlimited. Its members' mission is to "dethrone death," accept immortality into their DNA, and share it with those around them. When a member dies, the explanation is often that his or her belief in immortality was not strong enough. Ryan Van Velzer, "Immortality Eludes People: Unlimited Founder," azcentral.com, November 28, 2014, https://eu.azcentral.com/story/news/local/scottsdale/2014/11/16/people-unlimited-scottsdale-charles-paul-brown-immortality/19152253/.

3. Shlomo Breznitz, "The Seven Kinds of Denial," in *The Denial of Stress*, ed. Shlomo Breznitz (New York: International Universities Press, 1983), 257–80. See also Theodore L. Dorpat, *Denial and Defense in the Therapeutic Situation* (New York: Jason Aronson, 1985).

4. Breznitz, "The Seven Kinds of Denial," 34.

5. Emma Moersch, "Zur Psychopathologie von Herzinfarkt-Patienten," *Psyche: Zeitschrift für Psychoanalyse und ihre Anwendungen* 34, no. 6 (1980): 493–587.

6. I am grateful to Dr. Borut Jug for these observations.

7. Personal conversation with Chilean psychoanalyst Miguel Reyes Silva.

8. Ruth S. Shalev, "Anosognosia—the Neurological Correlate of Denial of Illness," in *Denial: A Clarification of Concepts and Research*, ed. Elieser Ludwig Edelstein, Donald L. Nathanson, and Andrew M. Stone (Boston: Springer, 1989), 119–24.

9. Edwin A. Weinstein and Malvin Cole, "Concepts of Anosognosia," in *Problems of Dynamic Neurology*, ed. L. Halpern (New York: Grine and Stratton, 1963), 254–73.

10. Weinstein and Cole, "Concepts of Anosognosia."

11. Catherine Morin, *Stroke, Body Image, and Self-Representation: Psychoanalytic and Neurological Perspectives* (London: Routledge, 2018).

12. Herman Musaph, "Denial as a Central Coping Mechanism in Counterhypochondriasis," in Edelstein, Nathanson, and Stone, *Denial*, 232.

13. Roger Higgs, "Truth Telling, Lying and the Doctor-Patient Relationship," in *Principles of Health Care Ethics*, ed. Richard E. Ashcroft et al. (Chichester, UK: John Wiley and Sons, 2007), 333–37.

14. Ruth R. Faden, Tom L. Beauchamp, and Nancy King, *A History and Theory of Informed Consent* (New York: Oxford University Press, 1986).

15. Tom L. Beauchamp, "Informed Consent: Its History, Meaning, and Present Challenges," *Cambridge Quarterly of Healthcare Ethics* 20, no. 4 (2011): 515–23; Peter M. Murray, "The History of Informed Consent," *Iowa Orthopaedic Journal* 10 (1990): 104–9.

16. Neil C. Manson, "Consent and Informed Consent," in Ashcroft et al., *Principles of Health Care Ethics*, 297–303.

17. Trudo Lemmens, "Informed Consent," in *Routledge Handbook of Medical Law and Ethics*, ed. Yann Joly and Bartha Maria Knoppers (Abingdon, UK: Routledge, 2014), 27–51.

18. Darian Leader and David Corfield have shown how medicine often overlooks the unconscious factors that are related to people's illnesses and how we often cannot find a rational explanation for why some people's illnesses only become apparent at the time of the anniversary of the loss of a loved one. See Darian Leader and David Corfield, *Why Do People Get Ill?* (London: Hamish Hamilton, 2007).

19. Justin Oakley, "Patients and Disclosure of Surgical Risk," in Ashcroft et al., *Principles of Health Care Ethics*, 319–24.

20. Merle Springs, "The Practical Limits and Value of Informed Consent," in *Informed Consent and Clinician Accountability: The Ethics of Report Cards on Surgeon*

Performance, ed. Steve Clarke and Justin Oakley (Cambridge: Cambridge University Press, 2007), 134–46.

21. Sally A. Santen, Robin R. Hemphill, Cindy M. Spanier, and Nicholas D. Fletcher, "'Sorry, It's My First Time!' Will Patients Consent to Medical Students Learning Procedures?," *Medical Education* 39, no. 4 (2005): 365–69.

22. Paul Kalanithi, *When Breath Becomes Air* (New York: Random House, 2016).

23. Sigmund Freud, "Thoughts for the Times on War and Death," in *The Standard Edition of the Complete Psychological Works of Sigmund Freud*, ed. James Strachey et al., vol. 14 (1914–1916), *On the History of the Psycho-Analytic Movement, Papers on Meta-psychology and Other Works* (London: Vintage Classics, 2001), 296.

24. Lacan thus says, "Death is never experienced as such, it is never real. Man is only ever afraid of an imaginary fear." Jacques Lacan, *The Seminar of Jacques Lacan*, bk. 1, *Freud's Papers on Technique*, ed. Jacques-Alain Miller, trans. John Forrester (New York: W. W. Norton, 1991), 223.

25. David A. Moskowitz and Michael E. Roloff, "The Existence of a Bug Chasing Subculture," *Culture, Health and Sexuality* 9, no. 4 (2007): 347–57.

26. With the success of antiviral drugs, some men who call themselves "bug-chasers" have started believing that HIV will be easy to manage. Since these men expect that they will get infected at some point in their lives, getting infected on purpose becomes a way to not worry anymore about what is to come. See Esben Elborne, "When HIV Is Considered a Gift," *Vice*, June 23, 2014, https://www.vice .com/da/article/mvnj3q/the-gift-of-hiv.

27. David Rieff, *Swimming in a Sea of Death: A Son's Memoir* (New York: Simon and Schuster, 2008).

28. David Rieff, "Why I Had to Lie to My Dying Mother," *Guardian*, May 18, 2008, https://www.theguardian.com/books/2008/may/18/society.

29. Elisabeth Kübler-Ross, *On Death and Dying* (New York: Macmillan, 1969).

30. Avery Weisman, *On Dying and Denying: A Psychiatric Study of Terminality* (New York: Behavioral Publications, 1972).

31. Camilla Zimmermann, "Denial of Impending Death: A Discourse Analysis of the Palliative Care Literature," *Social Science and Medicine* 59, no. 8 (October 2004): 1769–80.

32. Zimmermann, "Denial of Impending Death," 1773.

33. Zimmermann, "Denial of Impending Death."

34. Kathy Charmaz, *The Social Reality of Death: Death in Contemporary America* (Reading, MA: Addison Wesley, 1980).

35. Christine Colby, "You're Going to Die, Here's How to Deal with It," *Life-hacker*, February 1, 2017, https://lifehacker.com/youre-going-to-die-heres-how-to -deal-with-it-1791498957.

36. Sandra Laville, "Hans Kristian Rausing Kept Wife's Body Because He Felt 'Unable to Let Her Leave,'" *Guardian*, August 1, 2012, https://www.theguardian.com /uk/2012/aug/01/hans-kristian-rausing-wife-body.

37. Hannah Devlin, "The Cryonics Dilemma: Will Deep-Frozen Bodies Be Fit for New Life?," *Guardian*, November 18, 2016, https://www.theguardian.com/science /2016/nov/18/the-cryonics-dilemma-will-deep-frozen-bodies-be-fit-for-new-life.

38. Russ Banham, "The Departed: Communicating with Lost Loved Ones through AI and VR," Dell Technologies, December 4, 2019, https://www.delltechnologies .com/en-us/perspectives/the-departed-communicating-with-lost-loved-ones -through-ai-and-vr/.

39. Kristin Houser, "Watch a Mother Reunite with Her Deceased Child in VR: Would You Want to See a Deceased Loved One Again—in a Virtual World?," *Futurism*, February 7, 2020, https://futurism.com/watch-mother-reunion-deceased -child-vr.

Chapter 5

1. Jacques Lacan, *The Seminar of Jacques Lacan*, bk. 8, *Transference*, ed. Jacques-Alain Miller, trans. Bruce Fink (Cambridge: Polity Press, 2015).

2. Jacques Lacan, *The Seminar of Jacques Lacan*, bk. 1, *Freud's Papers on Technique*, ed. Jacques-Alain Miller, trans. John Forrester (New York: W. W. Norton, 1991), 271. If the symbolic has to do with the cultural setting in which we live, and especially the language we speak, and the imaginary concerns the images in which we observe ourselves and others, the real signifies the lack, the impossibility, what cannot be put into words, and also what involves people's unconscious desires and drives. In explaining the connection between love, hate, and ignorance, Lacan sketched a triangle in which he placed love at the corner where the symbolic meets the imaginary, hatred between the imaginary and the real, and ignorance between the symbolic and the real.

3. Michel Silvestre, *Demain la psychanalyse* (Paris: Navarin Editeur, 1987), 300; my translation.

4. Daphne du Maurier, *My Cousin Rachel* (New York: Little, Brown, 2013), https://www.ebooks.com/en-us/book/1564564/my-cousin-rachel/daphne-du -maurier.

5. Du Maurier, *My Cousin Rachel*.

6. William Shakespeare, "Sonnet CXXXVII," in *The Complete Works of William Shakespeare*, ed. William James Craig (Oxford: Oxford University Press, 1952), 1125.

7. William Shakespeare, "Sonnet CXXXVIII," in Craig, *The Complete Works of William Shakespeare*, 1125.

8. Russell Grieg and Justin Clemens, "A Note on Psychoanalysis and the Crime of Torture," *Australian Feminist Law Journal* 24, no. 1 (2006): 161–77.

9. Gilead Nachmani, "Trauma and Ignorance," *Contemporary Psychoanalysis* 31, no. 3 (July 1, 1995): 423–50.

10. Nachmani, "Trauma and Ignorance," 435.

11. Ruth R. Imber, "Clinical Notes on Masochism," *Contemporary Psychoanalysis* 31, no. 4 (October 1995): 581–89.

12. Arielle Pardes, "This Dating App Exposes the Monstrous Bias of Algorithms," *Wired*, May 25, 2019, https://www.wired.com/story/monster-match-dating-app/.

13. Jevan A. Hutson, Jessie G. Taft, Solon Barocas, and Karen Levy, "Debiasing Desire: Addressing Bias & Discrimination on Intimate Platforms," *Proceedings of the ACM on Human-Computer Interaction* 2, no. CSCW (November 2018): article 73, https://doi.org/10.1145/3274342.

14. Arielle Pardes, "Flirty or Friendzone? New AI Scans Your Texts for True Love," *Wired*, September 16, 2019, https://www.wired.com/story/ai-apps-texting -flirting-romance/.

15. Maya Kosoff, "You Have a Secret Tinder Rating—but Only the Company Can See What It Is," Business Insider, January 16, 2016, https://www.businessinsider.com /secret-tinder-rating-system-called-elo-score-can-only-be-seen-by-company-2016-1.

16. After being criticized for its "desirability score," Tinder claimed that it stopped using it. However, it still relies on secret algorithms in matching people that the company is not willing to reveal. See Steve Dent, "Tinder Ditches Its Hidden Desirability Scores," *Engadget* (blog), March 18, 2019, https://www.engadget.com/2019/03/18 /tinder-dumps-desirability-scores.

17. Clotilde Leguil, *"J"—une traversée des identités* (Paris: PUF, 2018), 111.

18. Danielle Knafo and Rocco Lo Bosco, *The Age of Perversion: Desire and Technology in Psychoanalysis and Culture* (London: Routledge, 2016), 129.

19. Alex Mar, "Modern Love: Are We Ready for Intimacy with Robots?," *Wired*, October 17, 2017, https://www.wired.com/2017/10/hiroshi-ishiguro-when-robots -act-just-like-humans/.

Chapter 6

1. Daisuke Fukuda, personal conversation with the author.

2. Susie Orbach, *Bodies* (London: Profile, 2009).

3. Stephanie J. Tobin, Eric J. Vanman, Marnize Verreynne, and Alexander K. Saeri, "Threats to Belonging on Facebook: Lurking and Ostracism," *Social Influence* 10, no. 1 (January 2, 2015): 31–42.

4. Fethi Benslama, *Un furieux désir de sacrifice: Le surmusulman* (Paris: Seuil, 2016).

5. Christina Cauterucci, "What These Deceptively Playful Memes Tell Us about Incel Culture," *Slate*, July 19, 2018, https://slate.com/human-interest/2018/07/incel -memes-like-millimeters-of-bone-and-virgin-vs-chad-mask-a-dangerous-and-toxic -culture.html.

6. Sigmund Freud, "Totem and Taboo," in *The Standard Edition of the Complete Psychological Works of Sigmund Freud*, ed. James Strachey et al., vol. 13 (1914–1916), *Totem and Taboo and Other Works* (London: Vintage Classics, 2001), vii–162.

7. Renata Salecl, *The Spoils of Freedom: Psychoanalysis and Feminism after the Fall of Socialism* (London: Routledge, 1994), 16, 17.

8. For a feminist critique of the incel movement, see Amia Srinivasan, "Does Anyone Have the Right to Sex?," *London Review of Books* 40, no. 6 (March 22, 2018), https://www.lrb.co.uk/the-paper/v40/n06/amia-srinivasan/does-anyone-have-the -right-to-sex.

9. Neil Strauss, *The Game* (Edinburgh: Canongate Books, 2011).

10. Rachel O'Neill, *Seduction: Men, Masculinity and Mediated Intimacy* (Cambridge: Polity Press, 2018), 154.

11. Helene Deutsch, "The Impostor: Contribution to Ego Psychology of a Type of Psychopath" (1955), in *The Mark of Cain: Psychoanalytic Insight and the Psychopath*, ed. J. Reid Meloy (Hillsdale, NJ: Analytic Press, 2001), 126.

12. Pauline Rose Clance and Suzanne Ament Imes, 'The Imposter Phenomenon in High Achieving Women: Dynamics and Therapeutic Intervention," *Psychotherapy: Theory, Research and Practice* 15, no. 3 (1978): 241–47.

13. MacDonald Critchley, *The Divine Banquet of the Brain and Other Essays* (London: Raven, 1970).

14. While most selfies are adjusted to enhance, improve, or embellish the "real image," special technology also exists to distort one's image. One can thus get an app that makes one look a different age or even preview how the face of an alcoholic could change after decades of drinking.

15. Deutsch, "The Impostor," 131.

Chapter 7

1. Btihaj Ajana, ed., *Metric Culture: Ontologies of Self-Tracking Practices* (Bingley, UK: Emerald, 2018).

2. Carl Cederström and Andre Spicer, *The Wellness Syndrome* (Malden, MA: Polity Press, 2015).

3. Jon Elster, *Sour Grapes: Studies in the Subversion of Rationality*, reissued ed. (New York: Cambridge University Press, 2016).

4. James Clawson, Jessica A. Pater, Andrew D. Miller, Elizabeth D. Mynatt, and Lena Mamykina, "No Longer Wearing: Investigating the Abandonment of Personal

Health-Tracking Technologies on Craigslist," in *UbiComp '15: Proceedings of the 2015 Association for Computing Machinery (ACM) International Joint Conference on Pervasive and Ubiquitous Computing* (New York: ACM, 2015), 647–58, https://dl.acm.org /doi/proceedings/10.1145/2750858.

5. James Clear, "The Akrasia Effect: Why We Don't Follow through on Things," *James Clear* (blog), January 11, 2016, https://jamesclear.com/akrasia.

6. Eric A. Finkelstein, Benjamin A. Haaland, Marcel Bilger, Aarti Sahasranaman, Robert A. Sloan, Ei Ei Khaing Nang, and Kelly R. Evenson, "Effectiveness of Activity Trackers with and without Incentives to Increase Physical Activity (TRIPPA): A Randomised Controlled Trial," *Lancet Diabetes and Endocrinology* 4, no. 12 (2016): 983–95.

7. Michael J. Sandel, *What Money Can't Buy: The Moral Limits of Markets* (2012; repr., New York: Farrar, Straus and Giroux, 2013).

8. Roy E. Baumeister, Ellen Bratslavsky, Mark Muraven, and Dianne M. Tice, "Ego Depletion: Is the Active Self a Limited Resource?," *Journal of Personality and Social Psychology* 74, no. 5 (1998): 1252–65.

9. Oliver Burkeman, "How to Keep Your Resolutions (Clue: It's Not All about Willpower)," *Guardian*, January 7, 2017, https://www.theguardian.com/lifeandstyle /2017/jan/07/how-to-keep-your-resolutions-not-all-about-willpower.

10. Kelly McGonigal, *The Willpower Instinct: How Self-Control Works, Why It Matters, and What You Can Do to Get More of It* (New York: Avery, 2012).

11. "Success Stories from the Pavlok Community," https://pavlok.com/success -stories/, accessed March 27, 2020.

12. Ashley Weatherford, "This New Hairbrush Is Totally Judging You," The Cut, January 4, 2017, https://www.thecut.com/2017/01/kerastase-and-withings-created -a-smart-hairbrush.html. The explanation is that the brush works in such a way that "three-axis load cells measure the pressure you exert on your hair and scalp as you brush, and sensors count the number and speed of brush strokes, and gauge if hair is being brushed wet or dry."

13. Robert Pfaller, *Ästhetik der Interpassivität* (Hamburg: Philo Fine Arts, 2009).

14. Pfaller expanded his theory to works of art. In exhibitions of contemporary art, it often happens that the visitor does not have an idea of what the works of art he or she is observing are all about. When walking around the exhibition, however, the person can have the impression that the curator somehow viewed the exhibition for them.

15. Amy Pittman, "The Internet Thinks I'm Still Pregnant," *New York Times*, September 2, 2016, https://www.nytimes.com/2016/09/04/fashion/modern-love -pregnancy-miscarriage-app-technology.html.

16. Pittman, "The Internet Thinks I'm Still Pregnant."

17. Laura Spinney, "Your DNA Is a Valuable Asset, So Why Give It to Ancestry Websites for Free?," *Guardian*, February 16, 2020, https://www.theguardian.com /commentisfree/2020/feb/16/dna-hugely-valuable-health-tech-privacy.

18. Nancy Tuana, "The Speculum of Ignorance: The Women's Health Movement and Epistemologies of Ignorance," *Hypatia* 21, no. 3 (August 1, 2006): 1–19.

19. Mark Andrejevic, "Big Data, Big Questions: The Big Data Divide," *International Journal of Communication* 8 (June 16, 2014): 1682.

20. On strategic ignorance, see Linsey McGoey, *The Unknowers: How Strategic Ignorance Rules the World* (London: Zed Books, 2019).

21. Richard Feldstein, Bruce Fink, and Maire Jaanus, eds., *Reading Seminar XI: Lacan's Four Fundamental Concepts of Psychoanalysis: The Paris Seminars in English* (Albany: State University of New York Press, 1995), 47.

22. Marc Dugain and Christophe Labbé, *L'homme nu: La dictature invisible du numérique* (Paris: Plon, 2016).

23. Toril Johannessen, "Words and Years," Toril Johannessen's website, http://www.toriljohannessen.no/works/words-and-years/, accessed March 27, 2020.

24. Ellen Dissanayake, "Komar and Melamid Discover Pleistocene Taste," *Philosophy and Literature* 22, no. 2 (1998): 486–96.

25. Clive Hamilton, *Requiem for a Species* (London: Routledge, 2015).

26. Deborah Lupton and Ben Williamson, "The Datafied Child: The Dataveillance of Children and Implications for Their Rights," *New Media and Society* 19, no. 5 (May 1, 2017): 780–94.

27. Andrejevic, "Big Data, Big Questions," 1674.

28. Rishabh Jain, "Coronavirus Update: China, Iran, Israel Mount Assault on Privacy with Surveillance, Location Tracking," *International Business Times*, March 16, 2020, https://www.ibtimes.com/coronavirus-update-china-iran-israel-mount-assault-privacy-surveillance-location-2940682.

29. A. J. Dellinger, "Ethicists Weigh In on the Implications of Using Phones to Track Coronavirus," Mic, March 17, 2020, https://www.mic.com/p/ethicists-weigh-in-on-the-implications-of-using-phones-to-track-coronavirus-22627285.

30. Noa Landau, Yaniv Kubovich, and Josh Breiner, "Israeli Coronavirus Surveillance Explained: Who's Tracking You and What Happens with the Data," *Haaretz*, March 18, 2020, https://www.haaretz.com/israel-news/.premium-israeli-coronavirus-surveillance-who-s-tracking-you-and-what-happens-with-the-data-1.8685383?=&ts=_1584565261668.

31. Noa Landau, "In Dead of Night, Israel Approves Harsher Coronavirus Tracking Methods than Gov't Stated," *Haaretz*, March 17, 2020, https://www.haaretz.com/israel-news/.premium-cellphone-tracking-authorized-by-israel-to-be-used-for-enforcing-quarantine-orders-1.8681979; Noa Landau, "Israeli Lawmakers Voiced Concerns over Tracking of Coronavirus Patients: The Government Ignored Them," *Haaretz*, March 17, 2020, https://www.haaretz.com/israel-news/.premium-israeli-government-ignored-lawmakers-concerns-over-tracking-of-coronavirus-patients-1.8684665.

32. Bernard Harcourt, *Exposed: Desire and Disobedience in the Digital Age* (Cambridge, MA: Harvard University Press, 2018).

Conclusion

1. Paul Radin, *The Winnebago Tribe* (Lincoln: University of Nebraska Press, 1990).

2. Claude Lévi-Strauss, *Structural Anthropology* (New York: Basic Books, 1963).

3. Steven Borowiec, "North Korea Says It Has No Coronavirus—Despite Mounting Clues to the Contrary," *Time*, March 3, 2020, https://time.com/5794280/north-korea-coronavirus/.

4. Irina Titova, "Doctors in Russia Are Accusing the Government of Covering Up Its Coronavirus Outbreak and Denying Them Protective Equipment," Business Insider, March 20, 2020, https://www.businessinsider.com/coronavirus-russia-doctors-say-government-is-covering-up-cases-2020-3.

5. Michael Rubin, "Gambling with 80 Million Lives: Why Erdoğan Lied about Coronavirus," *The National Interest*, March 16, 2020, https://nationalinterest.org/blog/middle-east-watch/gambling-80-million-lives-why-erdo%C4%9Fan-lied-about-coronavirus-133672.

6. Uri Friedman, "The Coronavirus-Denial Movement Now Has a Leader," *Atlantic*, March 27, 2020, https://www.theatlantic.com/politics/archive/2020/03/bolsonaro-coronavirus-denial-brazil-trump/608926/.

7. On "strategic ignorance," see Linsey McGoey, *The Unknowers: How Strategic Ignorance Ruins the World* (New York: Zed Books, 2019).

8. Julia Mastrioanni, "'Real People Won't Die': Rhetoric around Who Is at Risk of Coronavirus Infection Sparks Debate over Ageism, Ableism," *National Post*, March 3, 2020, https://nationalpost.com/news/world/real-people-wont-die-why-the-rhetoric-around-who-is-at-risk-for-coronavirus-is-so-harmful.

9. For a list of fake news, see Jane Lytvynenko, "Here's a Running List of the Latest Hoaxes Spreading about the Coronavirus," *BuzzFeed.News*, last updated March 24, 2020, https://www.buzzfeednews.com/article/janelytvynenko/coronavirus-fake-news-disinformation-rumors-hoaxes.

10. Michael Bang Petersen, Mathias Osmundsen, and Kevin Arceneaux, "A 'Need for Chaos' and the Sharing of Hostile Political Rumors in Advanced Democracies," conference proceedings, preprint, submitted September 1, 2018, https://doi.org/10.31234/osf.io/6m4ts.

11. Sigmund Freud, "Beyond the Pleasure Principle," in *The Standard Edition of the Complete Psychological Works of Sigmund Freud*, ed. James Strachey et al., vol. 18 (1920–1922), *Beyond the Pleasure Principle, Group Psychology and Other Works* (London: Vintage Classics, 2001); Jacques Lacan, *The Seminar of Jacques Lacan*, bk. 7, *The*

Ethics of Psychoanalysis 1959–1960, ed. Jacques-Alain Miller, trans. Dennis Porter (New York: W. W. Norton, 1997), 213.

12. Sean Adl-Tabatbai, "Millennials Caught Licking Toilets in Idiotic 'Coronavirus Challenge,'" NewsPunch, March 27, 2020, https://newspunch.com/millennials-caught-licking-toilets-idiotic-coronavirus-challenge/.

13. Jake Johnson, "'World Leaders Seem in Denial': Demands for Radical Global Action on Coronavirus as Virtual G20 Summit Ends with Vague Promises," *Pressenza,* March 27, 2020, https://www.pressenza.com/2020/03/world-leaders-seem-in-denial-demands-for-radical-global-action-on-coronavirus-as-virtual-g20-summit-ends-with-vague-promises/.

BIBLIOGRAPHY

Adl-Tabatbai, Sean. "Millennials Caught Licking Toilets in Idiotic 'Coronavirus Challenge.'" NewsPunch, March 27, 2020. https://newspunch.com/millennials -caught-licking-toilets-idiotic-coronavirus-challenge/.

Ajana, Btihaj, ed. *Metric Culture: Ontologies of Self-Tracking Practices.* Bingley, UK: Emerald, 2018.

Andrejevic, Mark. "Big Data, Big Questions: The Big Data Divide." *International Journal of Communication* 8 (June 16, 2014): 1673–89.

Aristotle. *The Metaphysics.* Buffalo, NY: Prometheus Books, 1991.

Arnold, Carrie. "'We Are All Mutants Now': The Trouble with Genetic Testing." *Guardian,* July 18, 2017. https://www.theguardian.com/science/2017/jul/18/we -are-all-mutants-now-the-trouble-with-genetic-testing.

Banham, Russ. "The Departed: Communicating with Lost Loved Ones through AI and VR." Dell Technologies, December 4, 2019. https://www.delltechnologies .com/en-us/perspectives/the-departed-communicating-with-lost-loved-ones -through-ai-and-vr/.

Barry, Ellen. "How to Get Away with Murder in Small-Town India." *New York Times,* August 19, 2017. https://www.nytimes.com/2017/08/19/world/asia/murder -small-town-india.html?action=click&module=RelatedCoverage&pgtype =Article&region=Footer.

Baumeister, Roy F., Ellen Bratslavsky, Mark Muraven, and Dianne M. Tice. "Ego Depletion: Is the Active Self a Limited Resource?" *Journal of Personality and So- cial Psychology* 74, no. 5 (1998): 1252–65.

Beauchamp, Tom L. "Informed Consent: Its History, Meaning, and Present Chal- lenges." *Cambridge Quarterly of Healthcare Ethics* 20, no. 4 (2011): 515–23.

Bellware, Kim. "White Woman Who Sued Sperm Bank over Black Baby Says It's Not about Race." Huffington Post, October 2, 2014. https://www.huffingtonpost.com /2014/10/02/black-sperm-lawsuit_n_5922180.html.

Benslama, Fethi. *Un furieux désir de sacrifice: Le surmusulman.* Paris: Seuil, 2016.

Bever, Lindsey. "White Woman Sues Sperm Bank after She Mistakenly Gets Black Donor's Sperm." *Washington Post,* October 2, 2014. https://www.washingtonpost

.com/news/morning-mix/wp/2014/10/02/white-woman-sues-sperm-bank-after-she-mistakenly-gets-black-donors-sperm/.

Bion, Wilfred R. *Seven Servants*. New York: Jason Aronson, 1977.

Borowiec, Steven. "North Korea Says It Has No Coronavirus Despite Mounting Clues to the Contrary." *Time*, March 3, 2020. https://time.com/5794280/north-korea-coronavirus/.

Breznitz, Shlomo. "The Seven Kinds of Denial." In *The Denial of Stress*, edited by Shlomo Breznitz, 257–80. New York: International Universities Press, 1983.

Brown, Zoe, and Marika Tiggemann. "Attractive Celebrity and Peer Images on Instagram: Effect on Women's Mood and Body Image." *Body Image* 19 (December 1, 2016): 37–43.

Burkeman, Oliver. "How to Keep Your Resolutions (Clue: It's Not All about Willpower)." *Guardian*, January 7, 2017. https://www.theguardian.com/lifeandstyle/2017/jan/07/how-to-keep-your-resolutions-not-all-about-willpower.

Caspi, Avshalom, Joseph McClay, Terrie E. Moffitt, Jonathan Mill, Judy Martin, Ian W. Craig, Alan Taylor, and Richie Poulton. "Role of Genotype in the Cycle of Violence in Maltreated Children." *Science* 297, no. 5582 (August 2, 2002): 851–54.

Cauterucci, Christina. "Sofía Vergara's Ex Might Finally Be Out of Luck in His Battle for Custody of Their Frozen Embryos." *Slate*, August 31, 2017. https://slate.com/human-interest/2017/08/sofia-vergaras-ex-might-finally-be-out-of-luck-in-his-battle-for-custody-of-their-frozen-embryos.html.

———. "What These Deceptively Playful Memes Tell Us about Incel Culture." *Slate*, July 19, 2018. https://slate.com/human-interest/2018/07/incel-memes-like-milli meters-of-bone-and-virgin-vs-chad-mask-a-dangerous-and-toxic-culture.html.

Cederström, Carl, and Andre Spicer. *The Wellness Syndrome*. Malden, MA: Polity Press, 2015.

Charmaz, Kathy. *The Social Reality of Death: Death in Contemporary America*. Reading, MA: Addison-Wesley, 1980.

Clance, Pauline Rose, and Suzanne Ament Imes. "The Imposter Phenomenon in High Achieving Women: Dynamics and Therapeutic Intervention." *Psychotherapy: Theory, Research and Practice* 15, no. 3 (1978): 241–47.

Clawson, James, Jessica A. Pater, Andrew D. Miller, Elizabeth D. Mynatt, and Lena Mamykina. "No Longer Wearing: Investigating the Abandonment of Personal Health-Tracking Technologies on Craigslist." In *UbiComp '15: Proceedings of the 2015 Association for Computing Machinery (ACM) International Joint Conference on Pervasive and Ubiquitous Computing*, 647–58. New York: ACM, 2015. https://dl.acm.org/doi/proceedings/10.1145/2750858.

Clear, James. "The Akrasia Effect: Why We Don't Follow through on Things." *James Clear* (blog), January 11, 2016. https://jamesclear.com/akrasia.

Cohen, Rachel, Toby Newton-John, and Amy Slater. "The Relationship between Facebook and Instagram Appearance-Focused Activities and Body Image Concerns in Young Women." *Body Image* 23 (2017): 183–87.

Colarusso, Calvin A. "Living to Die and Dying to Live: Normal and Pathological Considerations of Death Anxiety." In *The Wound of Mortality: Fear, Denial, and Acceptance of Death,* edited by Salman Akhtar, 107–23. Lanham, MD: Jason Aronson, 2010.

Colby, Christine. "You're Going to Die, Here's How to Deal with It." *Lifehacker,* February 1, 2017. https://lifehacker.com/youre-going-to-die-heres-how-to-deal-with -it-1791498957.

Critchley, MacDonald. *The Divine Banquet of the Brain and Other Essays.* London: Raven, 1970.

Cyr, Rachel E. "Testifying Absence in the Era of Forensic Testimony." *International Journal of Politics, Culture, and Society* 26, no. 1 (2013): 93–106.

Dallmayr, Fred. *In Search of the Good Life: A Pedagogy for Troubled Times.* Lexington: University Press of Kentucky, 2007.

Davis, William. *Nervous States: How Feeling Took Over the World.* London: Jonathan Cape, 2018.

Dean, Todd. "How to Measure What: Universals, Particulars and Subjectivity." In *On Psychoanalysis and Violence: Contemporary Lacanian Perspectives,* edited by Vanessa Sinclair and Manya Steinkoler, 127–34. London: Routledge, 2018.

Dellinger, A. J. "Ethicists Weigh In on the Implications of Using Phones to Track Coronavirus." Mic, March 17, 2020. https://www.mic.com/p/ethicists-weigh-in -on-the-implications-of-using-phones-to-track-coronavirus-22627285.

DeNicola, Daniel R. *Understanding Ignorance: The Surprising Impact of What We Don't Know.* Cambridge, MA: MIT Press, 2017.

Dent, Steve. "Tinder Ditches Its Hidden Desirability Scores." *Engadget* (blog), March 18, 2019. https://www.engadget.com/2019/03/18/tinder-dumps-desirability-scores.

Deraniyagala, Sonali. *Wave: A Memoir of Life after Tsunami.* London: Virago, 2013.

Deutsch, Helene. "The Impostor: Contribution to Ego Psychology of a Type of Psychopath" (1955). In *The Mark of Cain: Psychoanalytic Insight and the Psychopath,* edited by J. Reid Meloy, 115–32. Hillsdale, NJ: Analytic Press, 2001.

Devlin, Hannah. "The Cryonics Dilemma: Will Deep-Frozen Bodies Be Fit for New Life?" *Guardian,* November 18, 2016. https://www.theguardian.com/science/2016 /nov/18/the-cryonics-dilemma-will-deep-frozen-bodies-be-fit-for-new-life.

Dilley, Roy. "Reflections on Knowledge Practices and the Problem of Ignorance." *Journal of the Royal Anthropological Institute* 16 (2010): S176–92.

Dissanayake, Ellen. "Komar and Melamid Discover Pleistocene Taste." *Philosophy and Literature* 22, no. 2 (1998): 486–96.

Dorpat, Theodore L. *Denial and Defense in the Therapeutic Situation*. New York: Jason Aronson, 1985.

Dugain, Marc, and Christophe Labbé. *L'homme nu: La dictature invisible du numérique*. Paris: Plon, 2016.

Du Maurier, Daphne. *My Cousin Rachel*. New York: Little, Brown, 2013.

Dzidic, Denis. "Bosnia Discovers Two Wartime Mass Graves." *Balkan Transitional Justice*, June 9, 2015. https://balkaninsight.com/2015/06/09/bosnia-discovers-two-wartime-mass-graves.

Elborne, Esben. "When HIV Is Considered a Gift." *Vice*, June 23, 2014. https://www.vice.com/da/article/mvnj3q/the-gift-of-hiv.

Elster, Jon. *Sour Grapes: Studies in the Subversion of Rationality*. Reissued ed. New York: Cambridge University Press, 2016.

Faden, Ruth R., Tom L. Beauchamp, and Nancy King. *A History and Theory of Informed Consent*. New York: Oxford University Press, 1986.

Fardouly, Jasmine, Phillippa C. Diedrichs, Lenny R. Vartanian, and Emma Halliwell. "Social Comparisons on Social Media: The Impact of Facebook on Young Women's Body Image Concerns and Mood." *Body Image* 13 (March 1, 2015): 38–45.

Feldman, Sandor S. *Mannerisms of Speech and Gestures in Everyday Life*. New York: International Universities Press, 1959.

Feldstein, Richard, Bruce Fink, and Maire Jaanus, eds. *Reading Seminar XI: Lacan's Four Fundamental Concepts of Psychoanalysis: The Paris Seminars in English*. Albany: State University of New York Press, 1995.

Fenichel, Otto. *The Psychoanalytic Theory of Neurosis*. New York: Norton, 1996.

Feresin, Emiliano. "Lighter Sentence for Murderer with 'Bad Genes.'" *Nature*, October 30, 2009.

Finkelstein, Eric A., Benjamin A. Haaland, Marcel Bilger, Aarti Sahasranaman, Robert A. Sloan, Ei Ei Khaing Nang, and Kelly R. Evenson. "Effectiveness of Activity Trackers with and without Incentives to Increase Physical Activity (TRIPPA): A Randomised Controlled Trial." *Lancet Diabetes and Endocrinology* 4, no. 12 (2016): 983–95.

Firestein, Stuart. *Ignorance: How It Drives Science*. Oxford: Oxford University Press, 2012.

Freeman, Colin. "Ratko Mladic Walks out of Radovan Karadzic War Crimes Trial." *Telegraph*, January 28, 2014. https://www.telegraph.co.uk/news/worldnews/europe/serbia/10601233/Ratko-Mladic-walks-out-of-Radovan-Karadzic-war-crimes-trial.html.

Freud, Sigmund. "Beyond the Pleasure Principle." In *The Standard Edition of the Complete Psychological Works of Sigmund Freud*, edited by James Strachey et al., vol. 18 (1920–1922), *Beyond the Pleasure Principle, Group Psychology and Other Works*. London: Vintage Classics, 2001.

————. "Negation." In *The Standard Edition of the Complete Psychological Works of Sigmund Freud*, edited by James Strachey et al., vol. 19 (1923–1925), *The Ego and the Id and Other Works*. London: Vintage Classics, 2001.

————. "Thoughts for the Times on War and Death." In *The Standard Edition of the Complete Psychological Works of Sigmund Freud*, edited by James Strachey et al., vol. 14 (1914–1916), *On the History of the Psycho-Analytic Movement, Papers on Meta-psychology and Other Works*. London: Vintage Classics, 2001.

————. "Totem and Taboo." In *The Standard Edition of the Complete Psychological Works of Sigmund Freud*, edited by James Strachey et al., vol. 13 (1914–1916), *Totem and Taboo and Other Works*. London: Vintage Classics, 2001.

Friedman, Uri. "The Coronavirus-Denial Movement Now Has a Leader." *Atlantic*, March 27, 2020. https://www.theatlantic.com/politics/archive/2020/03/bolsonaro-coronavirus-denial-brazil-trump/608926.

Futrelle, David. "Why Are Incels So Obsessed with Other Men's Semen? The Answer Is Much Darker than You Think." *We Hunted the Mammoth* (blog), November 2, 2018. http://www.wehuntedthemammoth.com/2018/11/02/why-are-incels-so-obsessed-with-other-mens-semen-the-answer-is-much-darker-than-you-think/.

Giles, David C. *Twenty-First Century Celebrity: Fame in Digital Culture*. Bingley, UK: Emerald, 2018.

Gilovich, Thomas. *How We Know What Isn't So: The Fallibility of Human Reason in Everyday Life*. New York: Free Press, 1991.

Granel, Julio A. "Considerations on the Capacity to Change, the Clash of Identifications and Having Accidents." *International Review of Psycho-Analysis* 14 (1987): 483–90.

Grieg, Russell, and Justin Clemens. "A Note on Psychoanalysis and the Crime of Torture." *Australian Feminist Law Journal* 24, no. 1 (2006): 161–77.

Hamilton, Clive. *Requiem for a Species*. London: Routledge, 2015.

Harcourt, Bernard. *Exposed: Desire and Disobedience in the Digital Age*. Cambridge, MA: Harvard University Press, 2018.

Hartman, Tod. "On the Ikeaization of France." *Public Culture* 19, no. 3 (2007): 483–98.

Haun, Kathryn, and Eric J. Topol. "The Health Data Conundrum." *New York Times*, January 2, 2017. https://www.nytimes.com/2017/01/02/opinion/the-health-data-conundrum.html.

Higgs, Roger. "Truth Telling, Lying and the Doctor-Patient Relationship." In *Principles of Health Care Ethics*, edited by Richard E. Ashcroft, Angus Dawson, Heather Draper, and John R. McMillan, 333–37. Chichester, UK: John Wiley and Sons, 2007.

Hobart, Mark, "Introduction: The Growth of Ignorance?" In *An Anthropological Critique of Development: The Growth of Ignorance*, edited by Mark Hobart, 1–30. London: Routledge, 2004.

Hobson, J. Allan. *Dream Life: An Experimental Memoir*. Cambridge, MA: MIT Press, 2011.

Holmes, Jamie. *Nonsense: The Power of Not Knowing*. New York: Crown, 2015.

Hopkins, Jasper. *Nicholas of Cusa on Learned Ignorance: A Translation and an Appraisal of "De Docta Ignorantia."* Minneapolis: Arthur J. Banning, 1981.

Horowitz, Milton J. *Stress Response Syndromes*. Oxford: Jason Aronson, 1976.

Houser, Kristin. "Watch a Mother Reunite with Her Deceased Child in VR: Would You Want to See a Deceased Loved One Again—in a Virtual World?" *Futurism*, February 7, 2020. https://futurism.com/watch-mother-reunion-deceased-child-vr.

Huet, Natalie. "Relief and Justice for Relatives of Srebrenica." *Euronews*, November 22, 2017. https://www.euronews.com/2017/11/22/relief-and-justice-for-relatives-of-srebrenica-victims.

Hutson, Jevan A., Jessie G. Taft, Solon Barocas, and Karen Levy. "Debiasing Desire: Addressing Bias & Discrimination on Intimate Platforms." *Proceedings of the ACM on Human-Computer Interaction* 2, no. CSCW (November 2018): article 73. https://doi.org/10.1145/3274342.

Ibsen, Henrik. *The Wild Duck*. New York: Dover Thrift Editions, 2000.

Imber, Ruth R. "Clinical Notes on Masochism." *Contemporary Psychoanalysis* 31, no. 4 (October 1995): 581–89.

International Criminal Tribunal for the Former Yugoslavia. Trial of Radko Mladić, testimony on July 9, 2012. https://www.icty.org/x/cases/mladic/trans/en/120709IT.htm.

Jain, Rishabh. "Coronavirus Update: China, Iran, Israel Mount Assault on Privacy with Surveillance, Location Tracking." *International Business Times*, March 16, 2020. https://www.ibtimes.com/coronavirus-update-china-iran-israel-mount-assault-privacy-surveillance-location-2940682.

Johannessen, Toril. "Words and Years." Toril Johannessen's website. http://www.toriljohannessen.no/works/words-and-years/.

Johnson, Jake. "'World Leaders Seem in Denial': Demands for Radical Global Action on Coronavirus as Virtual G20 Summit Ends with Vague Promises." *Pressenza*, March 27, 2020. https://www.pressenza.com/2020/03/world-leaders-seem-in-denial-demands-for-radical-global-action-on-coronavirus-as-virtual-g20-summit-ends-with-vague-promises.

Kalanithi, Paul. *When Breath Becomes Air*. New York: Random House, 2016.

Kampschror, Beth. "Alija Goes Bye-Bye: Bosnia's President Retires Gracefully." *Central Europe Review* 2, no. 36 (October 23, 2000). https://www.pecina.cz/files/www.ce-review.org/00/36/kampschror36.html.

Kassam, Ashifa. "Sperm Bank Sued as Case of Mentally Ill Donor's History Unfolds." *Guardian*, April 14, 2016. https://www.theguardian.com/world/2016/apr/14/sperm-donor-canada-families-file-lawsuit.

Keller, Evelyn Fox. *The Century of the Gene*. Cambridge, MA: Harvard University Press, 2002.

Kerwin, Ann. "None Too Solid: Medical Ignorance." *Knowledge* 15, no. 2 (December 1, 1993): 166–85.

Khamis, Susie, Lawrence Ang, and Raymond Welling. "Self-Branding, 'Microcelebrity' and the Rise of Social Media Influencers." *Celebrity Studies* 8, no. 2 (April 3, 2017): 191–208.

Knafo, Danielle, and Rocco Lo Bosco. *The Age of Perversion: Desire and Technology in Psychoanalysis and Culture*. London: Routledge, 2016.

Knight, Sam. "Is a High IQ a Burden as Much as a Blessing?" *Financial Times*, April 10, 2009. https://www.ft.com/content/4add9230-23d5-11de-996a-00144feabdc0.

Kosoff, Maya. "You Have a Secret Tinder Rating—but Only the Company Can See What It Is." Business Insider, January 11, 2016. https://www.businessinsider.com/secret-tinder-rating-system-called-elo-score-can-only-be-seen-by-company-2016-1.

Kruger, Justin, and David Dunning. "Unskilled and Unaware of It: How Difficulties in Recognizing One's Own Incompetence Lead to Inflated Self-Assessments." *Journal of Personality and Social Psychology* 77, no. 6 (1999): 1121–34.

Kübler-Ross, Elisabeth. *On Death and Dying*. New York: Macmillan, 1969.

Lacan, Jacques. *The Seminar of Jacques Lacan*. Bk. 1, *Freud's Papers on Technique*. Edited by Jacques-Alain Miller. Translated by John Forrester. New York: W. W. Norton, 1991.

———. *The Seminar of Jacques Lacan*. Bk. 7, *The Ethics of Psychoanalysis, 1959–1960*. Edited by Jacques Alain-Miller. Translated by Dennis Porter. New York: W. W. Norton, 1997.

———. *The Seminar of Jacques Lacan*. Bk. 8, *Transference*. Edited by Jacques-Alain Miller. Translated by Bruce Fink. Cambridge: Polity Press, 2015.

———. *The Seminar of Jacques Lacan*. Bk. 10, *Anxiety*. Edited by Jacques-Alain Miller. Translated by A. R. Price. Cambridge: Polity Press, 2016.

———. "Some Reflections on the Ego." *International Journal of Psycho-analysis* 34, no. 1 (1953): 11–17.

Land, Greg. "Judge Dismisses Third Sperm Bank Lawsuit over Dodgy Donor." Law.com, February 26, 2018. https://www.law.com/dailyreportonline/2018/02/26/judge-dismisses-third-sperm-bank-lawsuit-over-dodgy-donor/?slreturn=20190901180157.

Landau, Noa. "In Dead of Night, Israel Approves Harsher Coronavirus Tracking Methods than Gov't Stated," *Haaretz*, March 17, 2020. https://www.haaretz.com/israel-news/.premium-cellphone-tracking-authorized-by-israel-to-be-used-for-enforcing-quarantine-orders-1.8681979.

Landau, Noa. "Israeli Lawmakers Voiced Concerns over Tracking of Coronavirus Patients. The Government Ignored Them." *Haaretz*, March 17, 2020. https://www .haaretz.com/israel-news/.premium-israeli-government-ignored-lawmakers -concerns-over-tracking-of-coronavirus-patients-1.8684665.

Landau, Noa, Yaniv Kubovich, and Josh Breiner. "Israeli Coronavirus Surveillance Explained: Who's Tracking You and What Happens with the Data." *Haaretz*, March 18, 2020. https://www.haaretz.com/israel-news/.premium-israeli -coronavirus-surveillance-who-s-tracking-you-and-what-happens-with-the-data -1.8685383?=&ts=_1584565261668.

Landrigan v. State. 1985 OK CR 52, 700 P.2d 218 (1985).

Lanzerath, Dirk, Marcella Rietschel, Bert Heinrichs, and Christine Schmäl. *Incidental Findings: Scientific, Legal and Ethical Issues*. Cologne: Deutscher Ärzte-Verlag, 2013.

Laub, Dori, and Nanette C. Auerhahn. "Knowing and Not Knowing Massive Psychic Trauma: Forms of Traumatic Memory." *International Journal of Psychoanalysis* 74, no. 2 (1993): 287–302.

Laville, Sandra. "Hans Kristian Rausing Kept Wife's Body Because He Felt 'Unable to Let Her Leave.'" *Guardian*, August 1, 2012. https://www.theguardian.com/uk /2012/aug/01/hans-kristian-rausing-wife-body.

Leader, Darian. *Why Do Women Write More Letters Than They Post?* London: Faber and Faber, 1997.

Leader, Darian, and David Corfield. *Why Do People Get Ill?* London: Hamish Hamilton, 2007.

Leguil, Clotilde. *"J"—une traversée des identités*. Paris: PUF, 2018.

Lehman, Andrée. "Psychoanalysis and Genetics: Clinical Considerations and Practical Suggestions." In *Being Human: The Technological Extensions of the Boundaries of the Body*, edited by Paola Mieli, Jacques Houis, and Mark Stafford, 201–10. New York: Marsilio, 2000.

Lemmens, Trudo. "Informed Consent." In *Routledge Handbook of Medical Law and Ethics*, edited by Yann Joly and Bartha Maria Knoppers, 27–51. Abingdon, UK: Routledge, 2014.

Lévi-Strauss, Claude. *Structural Anthropology*. New York: Basic Books, 1963.

Linder, Courtney. "Harvard Geneticist Wants to Build Dating App That Sure Sounds like Eugenics." *Popular Mechanics*, December 10, 2019. https://www.popu larmechanics.com/science/a30183673/dating-app-genetics.

Lupton, Deborah, and Ben Williamson. "The Datafied Child: The Dataveillance of Children and Implications for Their Rights." *New Media and Society* 19, no. 5 (May 1, 2017): 780–94.

Lytvynenko, Jane. "Here's a Running List of the Latest Hoaxes Spreading about the Coronavirus." BuzzFeed.News. Last updated March 24, 2020. https://www

.buzzfeednews.com/article/janelytvynenko/coronavirus-fake-news-disinfor mation-rumors-hoaxes.

Malone, Dan, and Howard Swindle. *America's Condemned: Death Row Inmates in Their Own Words*. Kansas City, MO: Andrews McMeel, 1999.

Mannoni, Octave. *Clefs pour l'imaginaire ou l'autre scène*. Paris: Seuil, 1985.

Manson, Neil C. "Consent and Informed Consent." In *Principles of Health Care Ethics*, edited by Richard E. Ashcroft, Angus Dawson, Heather Draper, and John R. McMillan, 297–303. Chichester, UK: John Wiley and Sons, 2007.

Mar, Alex. "Modern Love: Are We Ready for Intimacy with Robots?" *Wired*, October 17, 2017. https://www.wired.com/2017/10/hiroshi-ishiguro-when-robots-act -just-like-humans.

"Marko Pavić nazvao Dan bijelih traka 'slavljem' i 'gay paradom.'" Klix, June 1, 2013. https://www.klix.ba/vijesti/bih/marko-pavic-nazvao-dan-bijelih-traka-slavljem -i-gay-paradom/130601057.

Mašovič, Amor. "Genocid brez konca." Interview by Branko Soban. In *Zločin brez kazni*, by Branko Soban, 127–33. Ljubljana: Sanje, 2013.

Mastrioanni, Julia. "'Real People Won't Die': Rhetoric around Who Is at Risk of Coronavirus Infection Sparks Debate over Ageism, Ableism." *National Post*, March 3, 2020. https://nationalpost.com/news/world/real-people-wont-die -why-the-rhetoric-around-who-is-at-risk-for-coronavirus-is-so-harmful.

McGoey, Linsey. *The Unknowers: How Strategic Ignorance Rules the World*. New York: Zed Books, 2019.

McGonigal, Kelly. *The Willpower Instinct: How Self-Control Works, Why It Matters, and What You Can Do to Get More of It*. New York: Avery, 2012.

Meier, Evelyn P., and James Gray. "Facebook Photo Activity Associated with Body Image Disturbance in Adolescent Girls." *Cyberpsychology, Behavior and Social Networking* 17, no. 4 (April 2014): 199–206.

Mihajlović Trbovc, Jovana. "Memory after Ethnic Cleansing: Victims' and Perpetrators' Narratives in Prijedor." [Treatises and documents.] *Journal of Ethnic Studies* 72 (2014): 25–41.

Mills, Charles W. "Global White Ignorance." In *Routledge International Handbook of Ignorance Studies*, edited by Matthias Gross and Linsey McGoey, 217–27. London: Routledge, 2015.

Moersch, Emma. "Zur Psychopathologie von Herzinfarkt-Patienten." *Psyche: Zeitschrift für Psychoanalyse und ihre Anwendungen* 34, no. 6 (1980): 493–587.

Moore, Doug. "Bosnia: Bosnians in St. Louis Area Mark a Time of Trouble." STLtoday, April 4, 2012. https://www.stltoday.com/news/local/metro/bosnians-in-st-louis-area -mark-a-time-of-trouble/article_689876da-f739-5858-9444-04c2a5367749.html.

Morin, Catherine. *Stroke, Body Image, and Self-Representation: Psychoanalytic and Neurological Perspectives*. London: Routledge, 2018.

Moskowitz, David A., and Michael E. Roloff. "The Existence of a Bug Chasing Subculture." *Culture, Health and Sexuality* 9, no. 4 (2007): 347–57.

Mukherjee, Siddhartha. *The Gene: An Intimate History.* New York: Scribner, 2016.

Murray, Peter M. "The History of Informed Consent." *Iowa Orthopaedic Journal* 10 (1990): 104–9.

Musaph, Herman. "Denial as a Central Coping Mechanism in Counterhypochondriasis." In *Denial: A Clarification of Concepts and Research,* edited by Elieser Ludwig Edelstein, Donald L. Nathanson, and Andrew M. Stone, 231–35. Boston: Springer, 1989.

Nachmani, Gilead. "Trauma and Ignorance." *Contemporary Psychoanalysis* 31, no. 3 (July 1, 1995): 423–50.

Nettelfield, Lara J., and Sarah E. Wagner. *Srebrenica in the Aftermath of Genocide.* Cambridge: Cambridge University Press, 2014.

Oakley, Justin. "Patients and Disclosure of Surgical Risk." In *Principles of Health Care Ethics,* edited by Richard E. Ashcroft, Angus Dawson, Heather Draper, and John R. McMillan, 319–24. Chichester, UK: John Wiley and Sons, 2007.

O'Neill, Rachel. *Seduction: Men, Masculinity and Mediated Intimacy.* Cambridge: Polity Press, 2018.

Orbach, Susie. *Bodies.* London: Profile, 2009.

Orwell, George. *1984.* London: Penguin, 1956.

Panayotopoulos, Nikos. *Le gène du doute.* Translated by Gilles Descorvet. Paris: Gallimard, 2004.

Pardes, Arielle. "Flirty or Friendzone? New AI Scans Your Texts for True Love." *Wired,* September 16, 2019. https://www.wired.com/story/ai-apps-texting-flirting romance.

——. "This Dating App Exposes the Monstrous Bias of Algorithms." *Wired,* May 25, 2019. https://www.wired.com/story/monster-match-dating-app.

Pausch, Randy, and Jeffrey Zaslow. *The Last Lecture.* New York: Hyperion, 2008.

Perelberg, Rosine J. *Time, Space, and Phantasy.* London: Routledge, 2008.

Petersen, Michael Bang, Mathias Osmundsen, and Kevin Arceneaux. "A 'Need for Chaos' and the Sharing of Hostile Political Rumors in Advanced Democracies." Conference proceedings. Preprint, submitted September 1, 2018. https://doi.org/10.31234/osf.io/6m4ts.

Pfaller, Robert. *Ästhetik der Interpassivität.* Hamburg: Philo Fine Arts, 2009.

Pittman, Amy. "The Internet Thinks I'm Still Pregnant." *New York Times,* September 2, 2016. https://www.nytimes.com/2016/09/04/fashion/modern-love-pregnancy-miscarriage-app-technology.html.

Proctor, Robert N. "Agnotology: A Missing Term to Describe the Cultural Production of Ignorance (and Its Study)." In *Agnotology: The Making and Unmaking of*

Ignorance, edited by Robert N. Proctor and Linda Schiebinger, 1–35. Stanford, CA: Stanford University Press, 2008.

Radin, Paul. *The Winnebago Tribe*. Lincoln: University of Nebraska Press, 1990.

Raine, Adrian. *The Anatomy of Violence: The Biological Roots of Crime*. London: Allen Lane, 2013.

Raj, Suhasini, and Ellen Barry. "Indian Police Files Murder Charges after Times Describes Cover-Up." *New York Times*, September 18, 2017. https://www.nytimes.com/2017/09/18/world/asia/india-murder.html?searchResultPosition=1.

Renda, Matthew. "Judge Clears Sperm Bank Fraud Case for Trial." Courthouse News Service, March 31, 2017. https://www.courthousenews.com/judge-clears-sperm-bank-fraud-case-trial/.

Rieff, David. *Swimming in a Sea of Death: A Son's Memoir*. New York: Simon and Schuster, 2008.

———. "Why I Had to Lie to My Dying Mother." *Guardian*, May 18, 2008. https://www.theguardian.com/books/2008/may/18/society.

Roberts, Joanne, and John Armitage. "The Ignorance Economy." *Prometheus* 26, no. 4 (2008): 335–54.

Rogers, Katie, and Maggie Haberman. "Trump Now Claims He Always Knew the Coronavirus Would Be a Pandemic." *New York Times*, March 17, 2020. https://www.nytimes.com/2020/03/17/us/politics/trump-coronavirus.html.

Rubin, Michael. "Gambling with 80 Million Lives: Why Erdoğan Lied about Coronavirus." *The National Interest*, March 16, 2020. https://nationalinterest.org/blog/middle-east-watch/gambling-80-million-lives-why-erdo%C4%9Fan-lied-about-coronavirus-133672.

Salecl, Renata. *On Anxiety*. London: Routledge, 2004.

———. *The Spoils of Freedom: Psychoanalysis and Feminism after the Fall of Socialism*. London: Routledge, 1994.

———. *The Tyranny of Choice*. London: Profile Books, 2010.

Sandel, Michael J. *What Money Can't Buy: The Moral Limits of Markets*. 2012. Repr., New York: Farrar, Straus and Giroux, 2013.

Sanger, David E., and Nicole Perlroth. "A New Era of Internet Attacks Powered by Everyday Devices." *New York Times*, October 22, 2016. https://www.nytimes.com/2016/10/23/us/politics/a-new-era-of-internet-attacks-powered-by-everyday-devices.html.

Santen, Sally, Robin R. Hemphill, Cindy M. Spanier, and Nicholas D. Fletcher. "'Sorry, It's My First Time!' Will Patients Consent to Medical Students Learning Procedures?" *Medical Education* 39, no. 4 (2005): 365–69.

Schriro v. Landrigan. 550 U.S. 465 (2007).

Shakespeare, William. "Sonnet CXXXVII." In *The Complete Works of William Shakespeare*, edited by William James Craig, 1125. Oxford: Oxford University Press, 1952.

Shakespeare, William. "Sonnet CXXXVIII." In *The Complete Works of William Shakespeare*, edited by William James Craig. Oxford: Oxford University Press, 1952.

Shalev, Ruth S. "Anosognosia—the Neurological Correlate of Denial of Illness." In *Denial: A Clarification of Concepts and Research*, edited by Elieser Ludwig Edelstein, Donald L. Nathanson, and Andrew M. Stone, 119–24. Boston: Springer, 1989.

Silvestre, Michel. *Demain la psychanalyse.* Paris: Navarin Editeur, 1987.

Simpson, Joseph R. *Neuroimaging in Forensic Psychiatry: From the Clinic to the Courtroom.* Hoboken, NJ: John Wiley and Sons, 2012.

Son, Lisa K., and Nate Kornell. "The Virtues of Ignorance." *Behavioral Processes* 83, no. 2 (February 2010): 207–12.

Spinney, Laura. "Your DNA Is a Valuable Asset, So Why Give It to Ancestry Websites for Free?" *Guardian*, February 16, 2020. https://www.theguardian.com/commentisfree/2020/feb/16/dna-hugely-valuable-health-tech-privacy.

Springs, Merle. "The Practical Limits and Value of Informed Consent." In *Informed Consent and Clinician Accountability: The Ethics of Report Cards on Surgeon Performance*, edited by Steve Clarke and Justin Oakley, 134–46. Cambridge: Cambridge University Press, 2007.

Srinivasan, Amia. "Does Anyone Have the Right to Sex?" *London Review of Books* 40, no. 6 (March 22, 2018). https://www.lrb.co.uk/the-paper/v40/n06/amia-srinivasan/does-anyone-have-the-right-to-sex.

Strauss, Neil. *The Game.* London: Canongate Books, 2011.

"Success Stories from the Pavlok Community." Accessed March 2020. https://pavlok.com/success-stories.

Suzuki, Daisetz Teitaro. *Essays in Zen Buddhism: First Series.* London: Rider, 1958.

Tambiah, Stanley J. "The Magical Power of Words." *Man* 3, no. 2 (1968): 175–208. https://doi.org/10.2307/2798500.

Tedlow, Richard S. *Denial: Why Business Leaders Fail to Look Facts in the Face—and What to Do about It.* New York: Penguin, 2010.

Titova, Irina. "Doctors in Russia Are Accusing the Government of Covering Up Its Coronavirus Outbreak and Denying Them Protective Equipment." Business Insider, March 20, 2020. https://www.businessinsider.com/coronavirus-russia-doctors-say-government-is-covering-up-cases-2020-3.

Tobin, Stephanie J., Eric J. Vanman, Marnize Verreynne, and Alexander K. Saeri. "Threats to Belonging on Facebook: Lurking and Ostracism." *Social Influence* 10, no. 1 (January 2, 2015): 31–42.

Tuana, Nancy. "The Speculum of Ignorance: The Women's Health Movement and Epistemologies of Ignorance." *Hypatia* 21, no. 3 (August 1, 2006): 1–19.

Van Velzer, Ryan. "Immortality Eludes People: Unlimited Founder." azcentral.com, November 28, 2014. https://eu.azcentral.com/story/news/local/scottsdale

/2014/11/16/people-unlimited-scottsdale-charles-paul-brown-immortality
/19152253.

Ver Eecke, Wilfried. *Denial, Negation, and the Forces of the Negative: Freud, Hegel, Spitz, and Sophocles.* Albany: State University of New York Press, 2006.

Vilensky, Mike. "Live-Streaming Your Broke Self for Rent Money." *New York Times,* December 9, 2018. https://www.nytimes.com/2018/12/08/style/jovan-hill-live-stream-social-media-money.html.

Wajnryb, Ruth. *The Silence: How Tragedy Shapes Talk.* Crows Nest, New South Wales: Allen and Unwin, 2002.

Weatherford, Ashley. "This New Hairbrush Is Totally Judging You." *The Cut,* January 4, 2017. https://www.thecut.com/2017/01/kerastase-and-withings-created-a-smart-hairbrush.html.

Weinstein, Edwin A., and Malvin Cole. "Concepts of Anosognosia." In *Problems of Dynamic Neurology,* edited by L. Halpern, 254–73. New York: Grine and Stratton, 1963.

Weinstein, Edwin A., and Robert L. Kahn. *Denial of Illness: Symbolic and Physiological Aspects.* Springfield, IL: Charles C. Thomas, 1955.

Weisman, Avery D. *On Dying and Denying: A Psychiatric Study of Terminality.* New York: Behavioral Publications, 1972.

Witte, Marlys Hearst, Peter Crown, Michael Bernas, and Charles L. Witte. "Lessons Learned from Ignorance: The Curriculum on Medical (and Other) Ignorance." In *The Virtues of Ignorance: Complexity, Sustainability, and the Limits of Knowledge,* edited by Bill Vitek and Wes Jackson, 251–72. Lexington: University Press of Kentucky, 2010.

Zimmermann, Camilla. "Denial of Impending Death: A Discourse Analysis of the Palliative Care Literature." *Social Science and Medicine* 59, no. 8 (October 2004): 1769–80.

INDEX

academia, self-deception in, 15–16
agency: illness and, 78–79; work and, 80
agnosognosia, 82–94
AIDS, 90
akrasia, 130
Anatomy of Violence, The (Raine), 66–67
Andrejevic, Mark, 144–45
anxiety, 30, 69, 107, 111, 115, 129, 134; over appearance, 116; in coronavirus pandemic, 147; over death, 61; and denial of illness, 77–79, 90, 92; genetic testing and, 52–54, 62–63; impostor, 127; internet and, 29; over regard of others, 126; in war, 34, 43–44
apps: blockers for, 30; data tracking and, 139; dating, 53, 108–9, 168n16; epidemic control, 147; fitness, 133–34; health, 128–29; meditation, 134; pregnancy, 136
Arceneaux, Kevin, 153
Aristotle, 59–60, 130
Arlt, Peter, 111
Armitage, John, 28–29
art: data and, 141–43; exhibitions, 170n14; genetics and, 51; knowledge gaps and, 141
artificial intelligence, 109

authority: informed consent and, 86; in medicine, 85–86; skepticism of, 25–26; of social media influencers, 113–14

Barry, Ellen, 23–24
Baumeister, Roy, 131–32
Bayout, Abdelmalek, 66
Beierle, Scott P., 120
being ignored, 113, 127; emotion and, 98; incels and, 117–21, 124; love and, 106; relationships and, 106; social media and, 113–14, 116
belief(s): denial and, 19; and denial of illness, 91, 152; in expertise, 26; in forensic science, 46; genetics and, 64; ignorance and, in progress, 143–48; knowledge and, 101; love and, 101
Benslama, Fethi, 117
"beta men," 117–21
big data, 8; art with, 141–43; denial over, 135–38; informed consent and, 138–39, 145; self-monitoring and, 130–35; self-surveillance and, 128–30; surveillance and, 136–37; and trust in machines, 140–43
blind spots, 141–42
Bodies (Orbach), 116

industry and, 121–24; violence
against, 23–24, 118–19; in war,
47, 49
"Words and Years" (Johannessen),
141–42
work: agency and, 80; continuous,
122; glorification of, 80–81; and
"Ikeaization" of society, 25;

recovery from illness as, 81; as
refuge, 39
"wrongful birth," 55–59

Xi Jinping, 1

Zbanić, Jasmila, 45
Zen Buddhism, 21

A NOTE ON THE TYPE

This book has been composed in Arno, an Old-style serif typeface in the classic Venetian tradition, designed by Robert Slimbach at Adobe.